Great Meals in Minutes was created by
Rebus, Inc.
and published by Time-Life Books.

Rebus, Inc.

Publisher: Rodney Friedman
Editorial Director: Shirley Tomkievicz

Editor: Marya Dalrymple
Art Director: Ronald Gross
Managing Editor: Brenda Goldberg
Senior Editor: Charles Blackwell
Food Editor and Food Stylist: Grace Young
Photographer: Steven Mays
Prop Stylist: Cathryn Schwing
Staff Writer: Alexandra Greeley
Associate Editor: Ann M. Harvey
Assistant Editor: Bonnie J. Slotnick
Assistant Food Stylist: Karen Hatt
Photography Assistant: Glenn Maffei
Recipe Tester: Gina Palombi Barclay
Production Assistant: Lorna Bieber

For information about any Time-Life book,
please write:
Reader Information
Time-Life Books
541 North Fairbanks Court
Chicago, Illinois 60611
Library of Congress Cataloging in Publication Data

Italian menus.
   (Great meals in minutes)
   Includes index.
   1. Cookery, Italian.   2. Menus.
   3. Cooks—Biography.
I. Time-Life Books.   II. Series.
TX723.I84   1985   641.5945   84-28093
ISBN 0-86706-253-3 (lib. bdg.)
ISBN 0-86706-252-5 (retail ed.)

Time-Life Books Inc.
is a wholly owned subsidiary of

Time Incorporated

Founder: Henry R. Luce 1898–1967
Editor-in-Chief: Henry Anatole Grunwald
President: J. Richard Munro
Chairman of the Board: Ralph P. Davidson
Corporate Editor: Jason McManus
Group Vice President, Books: Reginald K.
Brack Jr.

Time-Life Books Inc.

Editor: George Constable
Executive Editor: George Daniels
Director of Design: Louis Klein
Board of Editors: Roberta Conlan,
Ellen Phillips, Gerry Schremp, Gerald
Simons, Rosalind Stubenberg, Kit van
Tulleken, Henry Woodhead
Editorial General Manager: Neal Goff
Director of Research: Phyllis K. Wise
Director of Photography: John Conrad Weiser

President: Reginald K. Brack Jr.
Senior Vice President: William Henry
Vice Presidents: George Artandi, Stephen L.
Bair, Robert A. Ellis, Juanita T. James,
Christopher T. Linen, James L. Mercer,
Joanne A. Pello, Paul R. Stewart

Editorial Operations
Design: Ellen Robling (assistant director)
Copy Room: Diane Ullius
Production: Ann B. Landry (director), Celia
Beattie
Quality Control: James J. Cox (director),
Sally Collins
Library: Louise D. Forstall

SERIES CONSULTANT
Margaret E. Happel is the author of *Ladies
Home Journal Adventures in Cooking*,
*Ladies Home Journal Handbook of Holiday
Cuisine*, and other best-selling cookbooks, as
well as the translator and adapter of Rebecca
Hsu Hiu Min's *Delights of Chinese Cooking*.
A food consultant based in New York City,
she has been director of the food department
of *Good Housekeeping* and editor of
American Home magazine.

WINE CONSULTANT
Tom Maresca combines a full-time career
teaching English literature with writing
about and consuming fine wines. He is now
at work on *The Wine Case Book*, which
explains the techniques of wine tasting.

Cover: Evelyne Slomon's antipasto, hearty
vegetable soup, and home-style pizza with
peppers. See pages 76–77

Great Meals
IN MINUTES
ITALIAN
MENUS

TIME
LIFE
BOOKS

TIME-LIFE BOOKS, ALEXANDRIA, VIRGINIA

Contents

Meet the Cooks

SILVANA LA ROCCA

The daughter of an Italian diplomat, Silvana La Rocca was born and raised in the Abruzzo region of central Italy. She has also lived in Rome and traveled extensively in Europe and South America. Although she holds a Master's Degree in international law, Silvana La Rocca cooks for a living. She resides in Berkeley, California, where she operates Made to Order, a delicatessen, take-out, and catering business.

FELICE AND LIDIA BASTIANICH

Felice Bastianich and his wife, Lidia, were born in Istria, but met and married in New York. They opened their first restaurant in Queens in 1970 and now own and operate Felidia in Manhattan, which features authentic Italian regional food with a focus on Istrian dishes.

LYNNE KASPER

Cooking teacher and food writer Lynne Kasper has studied with many leading cooks and at L'Ecole de Cuisine La Varenne in Paris. She is a founding member of the International Association of Cooking Schools, a former contributing food editor to *Denver Magazine*, and a regular contributor to *Bon Appétit* magazine. She now lives in Brussels, where she teaches cooking and is researching Italian culinary history.

SUSAN DeREGE

Born in Ontario, Canada, Susan DeRege is married to a native of Piedmont, Italy. She has traveled throughout northern Italy gathering unusual and authentic recipes and has worked as a test-kitchen home economist. Currently, she teaches food preparation at the New School Culinary Arts Program in New York City and at King's Cooking Studio in New Jersey.

NANCY VERDE BARR
A specialist in southern Italian cooking, Nancy Barr studied with Madeleine Kamman at Modern Gourmet in Massachusetts and also attended cooking classes given by Marcella and Victor Hazan and Giuliano Bugialli. She has taught cooking in France and at the Chefs Company Cooking School in Rhode Island and is executive chef to Julia Child on *Good Morning America* and at *Parade* magazine.

ROBERT PUCCI
Robert Pucci lives in Austin, Texas, and runs Pasta by Pucci, a catering business that specializes in Italian cooking. Besides catering, he works as a cook for several families. Interested in food since childhood, he lived in Italy for a year, studying and sampling the country's regional dishes. He is now working on a pasta cookbook.

EVELYNE SLOMON
Evelyne Slomon learned cooking in France. She is a charter member of the New York Women's Culinary Alliance and operates her own cooking school in New York City, which specializes in French and Italian cuisines and pizza workshops. She is the author of *The Pizza Book: Everything There Is to Know About the World's Greatest Pie.*

MAGGIE WALDRON
Maggie Waldron, a senior vice president and director of the Ketchum Food Centers in San Francisco and New York, works with major food clients worldwide. She studied cooking in Europe and Asia and attended classes at L'Ecole de Cuisine La Varenne in Paris. She is the author of several cookbooks, including *Barbeque & Smoke Cookery.*

JACK DENTON AND MARIA LUISA SCOTT
The Scotts have written 13 cookbooks, several of them best sellers, including *The Complete Book of Pasta, Mastering Microwave Cooking,* and *Feast of France,* which was written with French chef Antoine Gilly. Recent projects include *The Great American Family Cookbook* and *The Complete Meal-in-One Book of Pies.* Jack Denton Scott is a Commandeur Associé of the Commanderie des Cordons Bleus de France.

Italian Menus in Minutes

GREAT MEALS FOR FOUR IN AN HOUR OR LESS

Although many Americans identify Italian cooking with pepperoni pizza or spaghetti, these dishes are only a small sampling of the Italian repertoire. Italian cooking is so vast and diverse that it defies simple explanation. When Italians say *Mangia!* it means much more than "Eat!"—it expresses a unique love of food, cooking, and life.

The origins of Italian cooking can be traced back to the ancient Etruscans and Greeks. During the 500-year reign of the emperors, Roman cooking influenced that of the whole empire, and during the Renaissance, Italian cooking became the inspiration for most of the cuisines of Western Europe. Indeed, the culinary encyclopedia *Larousse Gastronomique* describes Italian cooking as the "veritable mother cuisine."

Italians prefer to think of their cooking in regional rather than national terms: Lombardian cooking, Ligurian cooking, or Sicilian cooking, for example. Part of the reason for this regionalism is that until 1870, when King Victor Emmanuel II united the country, Italy consisted of separate (often warring) states, each with its own traditions and cooking style. Even today, the regions (roughly corresponding to the former states) remain independent in spirit. Geography also separates the regions: The Appenine Mountains form a crooked spine that runs the length of the country, dividing and subdividing it into valleys, plains, plateaus, and coastal strips.

Despite this regionalism, Italian cooks do have a couple of things in common: a passion for pasta, which is served at practically every meal throughout the country; and an insistence on using only the very freshest ingredients purchased daily at local markets. Most Italian cooks also keep the same basic larder: cheeses, olive oils, wines, sausages, herbs, and garlic, which appear in one form or another in most dishes. Finally, Italian cooks share a love of simple food simply prepared. Italian cuisine would have to be described as *la cucina casalinga*—or home-style cooking.

A warm pizza with tomato sauce (top left) is one of thousands of Italian regional dishes. On the countertop are the components of many more. Clockwise from top left: Arborio rice, dried porcini mushrooms, pine nuts and plum tomatoes, Kalamata olives and garlic, artichokes, dried Italian sausage, pounded veal, Provolone, salami, angel hair pasta, green and white fettuccine, dried linguine, sun-dried tomatoes, thyme and rosemary, bell peppers, and a purple and white eggplant.

On the following pages, nine of America's most talented cooks present 27 complete menus with recipes that come from Italy or derive from Italian cooking. Each menu, which serves four people, can be prepared in an hour or less, and all have been adapted to American kitchens; yet each recipe retains the spirit of Italian regional fare, using fresh seafood and produce and good cuts of meat. Additional ingredients (vinegars, spices, herbs, and so on) are all of high quality and are widely available in supermarkets or occasionally in specialty food stores.

The cooks and the kitchen staff have meticulously planned and tested the meals for appearance as well as taste, as the accompanying photographs show: The vegetables are brilliant and fresh, the visual combinations appetizing. The table settings feature bright colors, simple flower arrangements, and attractive but not necessarily expensive serving dishes.

For each menu, the Editors, with advice from the cooks, suggest wines and other beverages. And there are suggestions for the use of leftovers and for complementary dishes and desserts. On each menu page, you will find a number of other tips, from an easy method for peeling and deveining shrimp to advice for selecting fresh produce.

BEFORE YOU START

Great Meals in Minutes is designed for efficiency and ease. This book will work best for you if you follow these suggestions:

1. Read the guidelines (pages 10–11) for selecting ingredients.

2. Refresh your memory with the few simple cooking techniques on the following pages. They will quickly become second nature and will help you to produce professional-quality meals in minutes.

3. Read the menus before you shop. Each lists the ingredients you will need, in the order that you would expect to shop for them. Many items will already be on your pantry shelf.

4. Check the equipment list on page 16. Good, sharp knives and pots and pans of the right shape and material are essential for making great meals in minutes. This may be the time to buy a few things. The right equipment can turn cooking from a necessity into a creative experience.

5. Set out everything you need before you start to cook: The lists at the beginning of each menu tell just what is required. To save effort, always keep your ingredients in the same place so you can reach for them instinctively.

6. Remove meat, fish, and eggs from the refrigerator early enough for them to reach room temperature.

7. Follow the start-to-finish steps for each menu. That way, you can be sure of having the entire meal ready to serve in an hour.

A GASTRONOMIC TOUR OF ITALY

The boot-shaped peninsula of Italy is segmented into 20 regions, which are subdivided into 94 provinces. Not only do Italians cook differently from one region to the next, but the provinces—and even the towns within them—have their own culinary idiosyncrasies. Nevertheless, differences between the cooking of the north and the south really divide Italian cuisine. Cooks in the prosperous industrial north, which is also dairy country, use butter as well as olive oil and prefer fresh egg-based pastas such as tagliatelli, lasagna, and ravioli. In the poorer south, cooks use less luxurious ingredients—olive oil and dried tubular pastas such as macaroni and spaghetti, which are made solely from flour and water.

The following brief tour begins in the north of Italy and moves south, highlighting the regions, provinces, and cities that have inspired the recipes in this volume.

North

Piedmont: At the base of the Alps, Italy's northwesternmost region has high mountains in the north, hills at its center, and rolling plains in the south. Not surprisingly, the rugged terrain and relatively cold climate have influenced Piedmontese cooking. This tasty, wholesome, heavy cuisine consists of boiled meats, polenta (cornmeal pudding or mush), soups, and rich desserts—a diet for a vigorous outdoor people. From the mountains, too, come the famed, delicate, white Piedmont truffles, *trifoli d'Alba*, prized for their rare perfume and flavor. From hillside vineyards come grapes for Barolo, Barbera, and Nebbiolo wines. On Piedmont's fertile plain—particularly along the Po River—farmers grow abundant crops of rice, onions, celery, artichokes, peppers, and asparagus. Piedmont's best-known cheese is Fontina. On page 37, Lynne Kasper offers a typical Piedmontese dish: peasant-style risotto (or creamy rice) with Italian sausage and fresh vegetables and herbs.

Liguria and *Genoa:* Just below Piedmont on the Ligurian Sea is the crescent-shaped region called Liguria, also known as the Italian Riviera. Its principal port, Genoa, influences the cooking of the entire region, with its focus on freshly caught seafood combined with aromatic herbs grown on the nearby hillsides. Basil, the best known of these Genoese herbs, is the basis for *pesto Genovese*, a cheese, garlic, and herb paste usually served in soups or spooned over pasta. Minestrone, a stew-like soup made with pasta, is another specialty of this region—in fact, the Genoese claim to have invented it, along with ravioli. Robert Pucci serves a Genoese dish of sautéed spinach with raisins and pine nuts, page 69, and Susan DeRege offers a Ligurian soup made with artichokes on page 52.

Lombardy and *Milan:* The fertile region of Lombardy, stretching from the Alps in the north to the Po Valley in the south, has a rich, diverse cuisine. This is dairy country and Lombardian cooks make lavish use of butter and cheese. They favor braising or stewing meats and vegetables, and relish the thick, flavorful sauces produced by these slow cooking methods. In Lombardy, every cook has a recipe for *risotto alla milanese* (rice braised with onions, butter, and saffron), and every family owns its own copper pot just for cooking polenta. Other regional specialties include the aperitif Campari, the sweet yeast cake *panettone*, aged balsamic vinegar, and the cheeses Bel Paese and Gorgonzola. On page 77, Evelyne Slomon prepares a Lombardian *fitascetta con peperoni*, one of the oldest styles of pizza in Italy.

Lombardy's capital city is Milan, a thriving commercial center with a cuisine that resembles classical French cooking with Austro-German overtones. Milanese cooks use herbs, tomatoes, and often wine to flavor their dishes. On page 102, Jack and Maria Scott offer a Milanese rice.

Venice: Once an important spice trading center, this fabled canal city in the region of Veneto (whose coastline curves around the Adriatic Sea) dictates the cuisine of its surrounding area. Like the city itself, Venetian food sparkles with brilliant hues and contrasting colors, yet it is basic: Variations on rice (usually prepared as risotto), beans, salt cod, and polenta, and, of course, fresh seafood are the usual fare. On page 86, Maggie Waldron prepares liver with sautéed onions, a dish for which Venice is famous.

Istria: Formerly part of Italy, this mountainous peninsula, now governed by Yugoslavia, projects into the northern Adriatic Sea. Istria is known for its seafood and game dishes, flavored with onions, garlic, and olive oil. Here the food is a blend of Austrian, Slavic, Hungarian, and Italian influences. Felice and Lidia Bastianich serve three Istrian-style meals, pages 27–33.

Emilia-Romagna and *Parma:* A rectangular region at the top of the boot of Italy, Emilia-Romagna is divided into Emilia in the north and Romagna in the south, with the regional and gastronomic capital, Bologna, roughly in the center. This fertile agricultural area on the Adriatic Sea offers a sumptuous cuisine replete with cheeses, pork products, meat and pasta combinations, and seafood specialties. Susan DeRege's Menu 1, page 46, offers a pasta dish called straw and hay (*paglia e fieno*) that is typical of the region.

The province of Parma in Emilia-Romagna is, after Bologna, one of the most interesting culinary areas of the region. Parma produces the famous grating cheese Parmesan (mentioned by Boccaccio in the *Decameron*) and the raw cured ham *prosciutto di Parma*, served throughout the world. Ham production is probably the most important business of the mountainous area around Parma. Jack and Maria Scott's Spaghettini with Two Cheeses, page 99, is a typical Parma offering.

Florence: The capital city of Tuscany, Florence offers a plain, traditional cuisine that is robust yet not heavy. When Italians think of Tuscany, they think of the succulent beef from Tuscan Val di Chiana cattle, which is featured prominently on Florentine menus, and of deep-fried meats and vegetables, grilled chicken, tripe, and bean dishes. No Florentine meal is complete without a glass of the renowned Chianti from grapes grown in the mountains between Florence and Siena. The Scotts prepare a Florentine salad of escarole with anise seeds and Gorgonzola, page 97.

Central

The Marches: The gentle climate of the Marches makes this an ideal agricultural area. Farmers raise sheep here, and the major crops are wheat, numerous varieties of fruit, corn, beets, and tomatoes. The rough peasant cuisine, which is based mainly on pasta, polenta, and locally grown vegetables, also features seafood dishes, notably *brodetto*, a chunky seafood stew similar to the French *bouillabaisse*. Lynne Kasper recalls the vegetable bounty of the Marches with her Minestrone with Chickpeas, page 43.

Rome: The political, religious, and gastronomic capital of Italy, Rome has a distinctive cosmopolitan cuisine that is influenced by the cooking of both northern and southern Italy and also by foreign cuisines. Romans use both flat and tubular pastas, cook with lard or bacon fat as well as olive oil and butter, and make extensive use of such cheeses as pecorino, mozzarella, and ricotta. Highly seasoned pork and lamb dishes (especially *abbacchio*, or roast suckling lamb) are Roman favorites.

Abruzzo: As it has always been, farming is still the major occupation for most inhabitants of Abruzzo, a mountainous region with a coastline on the Adriatic Sea. Here the cooking is simple, based on local produce. Goats and sheep graze on the mountain slopes and provide the milk for Abruzzo's cheeses, such as *scamorza* and *caciocavallo di pescocostanzo*, and pigs and lambs are raised for their meat. Major crops include wheat (usually made into the favorite local pasta, *macaroni alla*

A Guide to Olive Oils

Olive oils differ with the variety of olives, the climate and soil in which the olives are grown, and the method by which they are processed. The color of olive oil may vary from pale gold to jade green, but it is not an indication of quality. Any good oil, however, will have a distinct olive-like bouquet. Designations of quality vary from one country to another, and oil from the same producer may differ from year to year. Taste a number of oils and decide for yourself what you like. You may find you prefer a fruity Sicilian oil, a lighter Tuscan product, or perhaps one of the French, Greek, Spanish, or American oils. In any case, always choose a product labeled 100% OLIVE OIL, and look for one that is pressed where it is grown.

Traditionally, EXTRA-VIRGIN is the designation for olive oil of the highest quality. Although criteria vary, extra-virgin usually means that the oil is from the first cold pressing—without heat or further refining—of the finest hand-picked olives. Extra-virgin oil is low in acidity and therefore gentle on the palate. It is expensive but worth the price.

The less-expensive grades of oil—SUPERFINE VIRGIN and FINE VIRGIN—are good for everyday use and better for cooking than extra-virgin since they stand up better to heat. A general rule is to use the finest oils for salad dressings and delicate, uncooked dishes, or as an addition to cooked dishes such as soups, but only after they are removed from the heat. Use fuller flavored oils for robust sauces, meat dishes, and highly spiced foods.

Extra-virgin olive oil's fine flavor, low smoking point, and high cost make it unsuitable for frying. However, the lower grades of oil (those labeled simply PURE) are more refined and can safely be heated to about 400 degrees; this makes them usable for sautéing and even for deep frying. Remember, though, that olive oil will always add a distinctive flavor to the food cooked in it. In Italy today, the trend is to use olive oil only when it will noticeably enhance the food; if the oil's flavor will be negligible or overpowered by stronger seasonings, Italian cooks prefer to use a neutral vegetable oil.

Olive oil keeps well—for up to a year—if stored in a cool, dark place. Leave it in its original bottle or tin, tightly capped, or, if you prefer, decant a small amount into a smaller glazed ceramic or glass container (a half-size wine bottle is good) and keep it accessible for daily use. Do not use plastic containers, which may alter the taste of the oil. It is not desirable to refrigerate olive oil, as it will thicken and become difficult to pour.

chitarra), eggplant, and sweet and hot peppers. Along the coast fish dishes abound, often prepared with the white vinegar for which the region is known. Abruzzese cooks frequently lace their dishes with hot peppers. Silvana La Rocca was born and raised in Abruzzo. Her fillets of sole with tomatoes, basil, olives, and capers, page 23, and the peppered lamb chops and hunter-style potatoes, page 25, are adaptations of recipes popular in the region.

South

Naples: Neapolitan food—including pizza, mozzarella cheese, tomato-sauced spaghetti and macaroni—is the most universally familiar of all Italian regional cuisines. Neapolitan meals focus on pasta and seafood; meat does not play a large role here. Neapolitans eat well and never scrimp on desserts—their *gelati* (ice creams) and *granita* (ices) are renowned. Wines of the region include Falerno, Lacryma Christi, and Gragnano. Jack and Maria Scott prepare fedelini pasta with a spicy tomato sauce, a dish typical of Naples, on page 96.

Basilicata and *Apulia:* Situated at the southernmost tip of Italy, the mountainous agricultural region of Basilicata has a limited but hearty cuisine based on locally raised goats, lamb, pigs, and small game. Sausages, vegetables (particularly artichokes, cabbages, and hot peppers), the local cheeses Provolone and *caciocavallo*, and sweet pastries are also part of the diet. On page 56, Nancy Barr offers Braised Duck with Black Olives, a specialty of the region.

Neighboring Apulia is a region of fertile farmlands. Its capital city, Bari, a major port on the Adriatic Sea, has a rustic cuisine centered on pasta, bread, and seafood. Jack and Maria Scott's Menu 1, page 96, features whiting with clams, a popular dish in Bari.

Calabria and Catanzaro: The mountainous region of Calabria, the toe of the Italian boot, is surrounded on three sides by the sea and abuts Basilicata on the north. Pasta and vegetables are the region's mainstay. Eggplants and pimientos can be found growing everywhere, and fishermen provide the delicacies tuna and swordfish. Meals often consist of a simple fish soup and stewed or stuffed vegetables.

Calabria's capital city is Catanzaro, in the hills above the Ionian Sea. Catanzaro's cuisine features grilled and baked fish dishes, roast kid and lamb, vegetable soups thickened with pasta, and *morseddu*, a celebrated paste of pig giblets spread on bread. In fact, local bakers produce such large loaves of bread, it is said that one loaf can feed a family for a week. Nancy Barr's Calabrian Menu 1, page 56, includes penne (a quill-shaped pasta) and a mushroom sauce sparked with hot peppers, and she offers a lamb chop dish from Catanzaro on page 63.

Sicily: A mountainous island whose inhabitants cling to their ancient cooking traditions, Sicily is famous for its fertile lands, sunny climate, and spectacular scenery dotted with Greek ruins. Sicilians love food and eat with abandon, utilizing all that their farms and seas provide. Major crops include wheat, citrus fruit, figs, eggplant, peppers, tomatoes, broccoli, and squash. The people here eat little meat, but tuna, swordfish, mullet, sardines, and anchovies are staples. Cooks bake their own bread and serve tubular pastas with strongly seasoned sauces. Colorful, extremely sweet pastries made with cream, candied fruit, honey, and almonds usually conclude a typical Sicilian meal, along with Marsala, which is made only in this region. Evelyne Slomon serves a Sicilian-style pizza, page 79, accompanied by a fresh fennel and orange salad with pine nuts, lemon, and cinnamon.

THE ITALIAN LARDER (for this volume)

You will find that many of the ingredients necessary for preparing Italian meals are already in your refrigerator, on your pantry shelf, or available at the local supermarket. Those listed below are perhaps less well known, but also readily available.

Cured Meats and Sausages

Coppa: Pressed and dry-cured pork shoulder, also known as *capocollo*. Sold at Italian markets and in the delicatessen section of many supermarkets. Produced in spicy and mild versions.

Genoa salami: A strong-flavored pork sausage sometimes made with garlic and whole white peppercorns. Sold at most supermarkets.

Pancetta: An Italian bacon that is cured but not smoked. Can be bought by the slice at Italian markets and eaten without cooking.

Prosciutto: A dry-cured unsmoked ham with a dark pink color and mild flavor. Safe to eat without cooking. Because of import restrictions on raw pork products, prosciutto sold in the United States is produced here; however, it closely resembles the Italian product.

Sausages (sweet and hot): Italian link sausages, made from fresh pork and seasoned with fennel seeds, garlic, and red pepper for the hot type, are readily available.

Soppressata: A large, flat oval sausage of coarsely ground pork. Highly seasoned, sometimes with ginger.

Vegetables

Arugula: Also known as rocket or roquette. A pungent, peppery salad green with long, slender, lobed leaves. Because of its slightly bitter aftertaste, arugula is best mixed with other salad greens. Select bunches that are bright green, fresh looking, and unwilted.

Broccoli rabe: Also called *broccoli di rabe* or rabe. A sharp-flavored green of the cabbage family, it does not taste like broccoli. Has long edible stems, narrow serrated leaves, and small bud clusters. Look for fresh springy leaves and stems.

Finocchio: Also known as fennel, Florence fennel, or anise. Resembles a flattened bunch of celery with a bulbous base, long white stalk, and feathery green leaves. Has a distinctive yet faint taste of licorice. A fall-winter vegetable, it does not keep well, so buy it just before you plan to use it. Select firm unblemished bulbs.

Radicchio: A wild chicory with short heart-shaped ruby-red leaves, prized as a salad vegetable. Available in fall and winter, it should be stored like lettuce.

Swiss chard: A member of the beet family, Swiss chard, or chard, has long leaves that resemble spinach and white or red ribs; both parts are edible. A summer-fall vegetable, but often hard to find in stores; it grows well in gardens. Like all greens, its leaves should be fresh and crisp; smaller leaves are younger and more tender.

Cheese

Asiago: A hard Cheddar-type cheese with a sharp tang, light-yellow color, and firm texture. Suitable for the table when young, and good for grating when aged.

Bel Paese: Soft, creamy, and mild. One of Italy's finest soft cheeses, made in Lombardy.

Caciocavallo: "Cheese on horseback"—probably named because its shape resembles saddlebags. A firm cheese suitable for grating when aged. When young, it is springy like mozzarella.

Fontina: Bland, buttery, and similar to mild Swiss. Its ivory interior, dotted with small holes, has a firm yet supple texture, suited to grating and melting.

Gorgonzola: Italy's version of blue cheese; rich, firm, and pungent. Delicious with fruits, as a sandwich filling, or crumbled into a salad.

Mozzarella: Once made from the milk of water buffalo, but today mainly a cow's-milk product. Sold unripened, so its flavor is mild and almost sweet. A pure white cheese prized for its melting qualities.

Parmesan: Italy's most popular grating cheese, best when freshly grated. Pale straw-yellow in color, aged Parmesan is dry and granular and will last almost indefinitely. The finest Parmesan is labeled Parmigiano-Reggiano and comes from the area around Parma.

Pecorino Romano: A hard-textured, sharp-flavored cheese suitable for grating when aged.

Ricotta: A soft white fresh cheese similar to cottage cheese; well suited for use in sweet and savory dishes. Available as a whole- or skimmed-milk product.

Beans, Corn, and Rice

Beans: Dried beans are used frequently in Italian recipes. A few common varieties included in this volume are chickpeas, borlotti, and cannellini. Chickpeas (known as *ceci* in Italy) come canned or dried at most supermarkets. Pale yellow, they are good in soups, stews, and salads. Borlotti are pink with red speckles and are similar to the American pinto bean. Cannellini, a white variety of kidney beans, are imported dried or canned from Italy. Substitute Great Northern or Navy beans.

Corn: To make polenta, white and yellow corn (ground coarse, medium, or fine) is cooked with water, milk, broth, or even wine, and served soft or solid. American white stoneground cornmeal can be used. If you substitute American yellow cornmeal, use 1⅓ cups for each 1 cup of polenta meal specified.

Rice: Arborio is the generic name for a pearly variety of short, round rice grown in northern Italy and preferred for risotto (in this volume long-grain rice is occasionally used). Arborio is sold at specialty food stores, Italian groceries, and some supermarkets.

A Glossary of Pasta in This Volume

Over the centuries Italian pasta makers have cut, molded, pressed, twisted, and extruded pasta into every conceivable form—an estimated 600 different shapes in all. The glossary below lists the pasta used in this volume.

Capelli d'angelo (angel hair)
Fine, flat pasta only a fraction as thick as spaghetti; angel hair cooks almost as soon as you immerse it in boiling water.

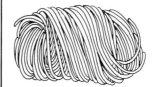

Capellini (fine hairs)
A very fine pasta as slender as capelli d'angelo but round. Fresh capellini may cook in less than a minute.

Fedelini
The thinnest of all spaghettis, sold twisted into "nests."

Fettuccine (small ribbons)
These flat noodles, about one-quarter-inch wide, are especially good fresh—and are the easiest pasta to buy that way.

Linguine (small tongues)
This long, flat pasta is well suited to relatively liquid sauces.

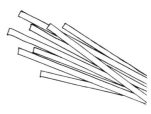

Pappardelle
These are broad egg noodles with ruffled edges. The Italians often serve these noodles with hare.

Penne (quills)
Usually smooth (though some types are grooved), these small pasta tubes are cut on the diagonal at each end.

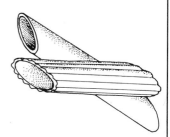

Spaghettini
A thin form of spaghetti, spaghettini is excellent with vegetable or seafood sauces.

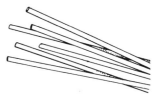

GENERAL COOKING TECHNIQUES

Sautéing

Sautéing is a form of quick frying, with no cover on the pan. In French, *sauter* means "to jump," which is what vegetables or small pieces of food do when you shake the sauté pan. The purpose is to brown the food lightly and seal in the juices, sometimes before further cooking. This technique has three critical elements: the right pan, the proper temperature, and dry food.

The sauté pan: A proper sauté pan is 10 to 12 inches in diameter and has 2- to 3-inch straight sides; it allows you to turn the food and still keep the fat from spattering. It has a heavy bottom that can be moved back and forth easily across a burner.

The best material (and the most expensive) for a sauté pan is tin-lined copper because it is a superior heat conductor. Heavy-gauge cast aluminum works well but will discolor acidic food like tomatoes. Another option is to select a heavy-duty sauté pan made of strong, heat-conducting aluminum alloys. This type of professional cookware is smooth and stick resistant. Be sure you buy a sauté pan with a handle that is long and comfortable to hold, and with a tight-fitting cover, since many recipes call for covered cooking following the initial sautéing.

Use a sauté pan large enough to hold the food without crowding, or sauté in two batches. The heat of the fat and the air spaces between the pieces facilitate browning. Crowding results in steaming, which releases juices.

Keep the food moving in the pan by using a wooden spatula or tongs as you shake the pan over the burner. If the food sticks, as it occasionally will, a metal spatula will loosen it best. Turn the food so that all surfaces come into contact with the hot fat. Do not use a fork when sautéing meat; piercing the meat will allow the juices to escape.

The fat: Half butter and half vegetable oil is perfect for most sautéing: It heats to high temperatures without burning, yet allows a rich butter flavor.

If you prefer an all-butter flavor, clarify the butter before you begin. This means removing the milk solids (which scorch easily) from the oils. To clarify butter, heat it in a small heavy saucepan over medium heat and, using a cooking spoon, skim off and discard the foam as it rises to the top. Keep skimming until no more foam appears. Pour off the remaining liquid, which is the clarified butter, leaving the milky residue at the bottom of the pan.

Some sautéing recipes in this book call for olive oil, which imparts a delicious and distinctive flavor of its own and is less sensitive than butter to high heat. Nevertheless, olive oil will occasionally scorch. Watch carefully when you sauté in olive oil; discard any scorched oil and start with fresh, if necessary.

To sauté properly, heat the fat until it is hot but not smoking. When you see small bubbles on top of the fat, lower the heat because it is on the verge of smoking. When using butter and oil together, add butter to the hot oil. After the foam from the melting butter subsides, you are ready to sauté. If the temperature of the fat is just right, the food will sizzle when you put it in the pan.

Pizza

Pizza evolved from the hearth-baked flatbreads of ancient times, but the Italians have refined it and elaborated upon it. Today, the varieties are endless: Flat, rolled, folded, or stuffed, pizzas can have almost any kind of filling.

Evelyne Slomon, whose recipes for food-processor pizza dough appear on pages 76–83, has provided the following traditional method for making the dough.

Pizza Dough by Hand

1 cup hot tap water
1 package active dry yeast
3½ cups all-purpose white flour, approximately
½ teaspoon salt
Vegetable oil for greasing bowl

1. In medium-size mixing bowl, combine hot tap water with yeast, stirring gently with fork until yeast has dissolved and liquid turns light beige.

2. Add 1 cup flour and salt, and stir with a wooden spoon to combine. Add another cup of flour and mix until dough starts to pull away from sides of bowl and begins to form a soft, sticky mass.

3. Sprinkle some flour over work surface and flour your hands generously. Remove dough from bowl and knead in another cup of flour, one-quarter cup at a time.

4. With heel of one hand (or both hands, if you wish), push dough across floured work surface. Grab dough with one hand and twist and fold it over. Scrape up any moist dough that sticks to work surface. Working quickly, repeat this action,

adding only as much of remaining flour as it takes to keep dough from sticking to your hands.

5. To test, push the heel of your hand into dough for 10 seconds. If your hand comes up clean, the dough is ready; if it is sticky, a bit more kneading will be necessary. Be careful not to overwork the dough; continue kneading only until it is smooth and elastic, about 5 to 10 minutes.

6. Clean the bowl and lightly grease it with vegetable oil. Place dough in bowl and turn dough until evenly coated with a thin film of oil. Cover bowl securely with plastic wrap.

7. Let dough rise 30 to 45 minutes in a warm, draft-free place, preferably in a gas oven with a pilot light or in an electric oven preheated to 200 degrees and then turned off.

8. Once dough has doubled in bulk, punch it down with your fist and turn it onto a lightly floured surface and knead it for another minute. Follow your recipe for what to do next.

Advance Preparation of Pizza Dough

Refrigerated rising: To prepare pizza dough a day ahead, follow the recipe above through step 6, and refrigerate dough. The next morning, punch dough down and knead it for 1 minute. Return dough to bowl, reseal, and refrigerate. Be sure to remove dough from refrigerator at least 30 minutes before rolling it out.

Freezing: After step 6 above, press dough into ½-inch-thick disk, wrap in plastic, and freeze. Defrost dough for 6 to 8 hours in refrigerator or set it in a warm place for 2 hours. Use the dough as soon as it is warm enough to handle. Although the dough will not be double in bulk, follow step 8.

Deglazing

Deglazing is an easy way to create a sauce for sautéed, braised, or roasted food. To deglaze a pan, pour off all but 1 or 2 tablespoons of the fat in which the food has been cooked. Add liquid—water, wine, or stock—and reduce the sauce over medium heat, using a wooden spoon to scrape the concentrated juices and brown bits of food clinging to the bottom of the pan. The Bastianiches use this technique in Menu 3, page 33.

Stir Frying

The basic cooking method for Chinese cuisine, this fast-cook technique requires very little oil, and the foods—which you stir continuously—fry quickly over a very high heat. Stir frying is ideal for cooking bite-size, shredded, or thinly sliced portions of vegetables, fish, meat, or poultry, alone or in combination. Evelyne Slomon stir fries spinach, page 77.

Braising

Braising is simmering meats or vegetables in a relatively small amount of liquid, usually for a long period of time. Occasionally, foods that do not need tenderizing may be braised more quickly to impart flavor. Sometimes the food is browned or parboiled before braising. You may wish to flavor the braising liquid with herbs, spices, and aromatic vegetables, or use wine, stock, or tomato sauce. Robert Pucci braises beef tenderloin in wine, page 66.

Glazing

Glazing vegetables in their cooking liquid, butter, and a little sugar gives them a slight sheen as the butter and sugar reduce to a syrupy consistency. Glazing enhances the vegetables' flavor and appearance, and they need no additional sauce. Instead of using sugar, Susan DeRege glazes carrots in a sweet cherry liqueur, page 47.

Blanching

Also called parboiling, blanching is an invaluable technique. Immerse whole or cut vegetables for a few moments in boiling water, then "refresh" them—that is, plunge them into cold water to stop their cooking and set their colors. Blanching softens or tenderizes dense or crisp vegetables, often as a preliminary to further cooking by another method, such as stir frying. Nancy Barr blanches broccoli rabe, page 63.

Poaching

You poach meat, fish, chicken, fruit, and eggs in very hot liquid in a pan on top of the stove. You can use water or, better still, beef, chicken, or fish stock, or a combination of stock and white wine, or even cream as the poaching liquid. Jack and Maria Scott poach whiting in wine, page 97.

Roasting and Baking

Roasting is a dry-heat process, usually used for large cuts of meat and poultry, that cooks the food by exposing it to heated air in an oven or, perhaps, a covered barbecue. For more even circulation of heat, the food should be placed in a shallow pan or on a rack in a pan. For greater moisture retention, baste the food with its own juices, fat, or a flavorful marinade.

Baking applies to the dry-heat cooking of foods such as casseroles; small cuts of meat, fish, and poultry; vegetables; and, of course, breads and pastries. Some foods are baked tightly covered to retain their juices and flavors; others, such as breads, cakes, and cookies, are baked in open pans to release moisture. Evelyne Slomon bakes pizza and two pizza variations, pages 75–83.

Broiling and Grilling

These are two relatively fast ways to cook meat, poultry, and fish, giving food a crisp exterior while leaving the inside juicy. Whether broiling or grilling, brush the food with melted fat, a sauce, or marinade before you cook. This adds flavor and moisture.

In broiling, the food cooks directly under the heat source. In grilling, the food cooks either directly over an open fire or on a well-seasoned cast-iron or stoneware griddle placed directly over a burner. Lynne Kasper broils a butterflied leg of lamb, page 40.

Making Stock

Although canned chicken broth or stock is all right for emergencies, homemade chicken stock has a rich flavor that is hard to match. Moreover, the commercial broths—particularly the canned ones—are likely to be oversalted.

To make your own stock, save chicken parts as they accumulate and put them in a bag in the freezer; then have a rainy-day stock-making session, using the recipe below. The skin from a yellow onion will add color; the optional veal bone will add extra flavor and richness to the stock.

Basic Chicken Stock

3 pounds bony chicken parts, such as wings, back, and neck
1 veal knuckle (optional)
3 quarts cold water
1 yellow unpeeled onion, stuck with 2 cloves
2 stalks celery with leaves, cut in two
12 crushed peppercorns
2 carrots, scraped and cut into 2-inch lengths
4 sprigs parsley
1 bay leaf
1 tablespoon fresh thyme, or 1 teaspoon dried
Salt (optional)

1. Wash chicken parts and veal knuckle (if you are using it) and drain. Place in large soup kettle or stockpot (any big pot) with the remaining ingredients—except salt. Cover pot and bring to a boil over medium heat.

2. Lower heat and simmer stock, partly covered, 2 to 3 hours. Skim foam and scum from top of stock several times. Add salt to taste after stock has cooked 1 hour.

3. Strain stock through fine sieve placed over large bowl. Discard solids. Let stock cool uncovered (this will speed cooling process). When completely cool, refrigerate. Fat will rise and congeal conveniently at top. You may skim it off and discard it or leave it as a protective covering.

Yield: About 10 cups

Pantry (for this volume)

A well-stocked, properly organized pantry is essential for preparing great meals in the shortest time possible. Whether your pantry consists of a small refrigerator and two or three shelves over the sink, or a large freezer, refrigerator, and entire room just off the kitchen, you must protect staples from heat and light.

In maintaining your pantry, follow these rules:

1. Store staples by kind and date. Canned goods, canisters, and spices need a separate shelf, or a separate spot on a shelf. Date all staples—shelved, refrigerated, or frozen—by writing the date directly on the package or on a bit of masking tape. Then put the oldest ones in front to be sure you use them first.

2. Store flour, sugar, and other dry ingredients in canisters or jars with tight lids. Glass and clear plastic allow you to see at a glance how much remains.

3. Keep a running grocery list so that you can note when a staple is half gone, and be sure to stock up.

ON THE SHELF:

Anchovies
Anchovy fillets, both flat and rolled, come oil-packed, in tins. If you buy whole, salt-packed anchovies, they must be cleaned under running water, skinned, and boned. To bone, separate the fish with your fingers and slip out the backbone.

Capers
Capers are usually packed in vinegar and less frequently in salt. If you use the latter, you should rinse them under cold water before using them.

Flour
all-purpose, bleached or unbleached
cornmeal
May be yellow or white and of various degrees of coarseness. The stone-ground variety, milled to retain the germ of the corn, generally has a superior flavor.

Dried fruits
Golden raisins

Garlic
Store in a cool, dry, well-ventilated place. Garlic powder and garlic salt are not adequate substitutes for fresh garlic.

Herbs and spices
The flavor of fresh herbs is much better than that of dried. Fresh herbs should be refrigerated and used as soon as possible. The following herbs are perfectly acceptable dried, but buy in small amounts, store airtight in dry area away from heat and light, and use as quickly as possible. In measuring herbs, remember that one part dried will equal three parts fresh. *Note:* Dried chives and parsley should not be on your shelf, since they have little or no flavor; frozen chives are acceptable. Buy whole spices rather than ground, as they keep their flavor much longer. Grind spices at home and store as directed for herbs.

basil
bay leaves
Cayenne pepper
cinnamon
cloves, whole and ground
fennel seeds
marjoram
mint
mustard (powdered)
nutmeg, whole and ground
oregano
pepper
　black peppercorns
　These are unripe peppercorns dried in their husks. Grind with a pepper mill for each use.
　white peppercorns
　These are the same as the black variety, but are picked ripe and husked. Use them in pale sauces when black pepper specks would spoil the appearance.
red pepper flakes (also called crushed red pepper)
rosemary
saffron
Made from the dried stigmas of a species of crocus, this spice—the most costly of all seasonings—adds both color and flavor. Use sparingly.
sage
salt
Use coarse salt—commonly available as Kosher or sea—for its superior flavor, texture, and purity. Kosher salt and sea salt are less salty than table salt. Substitute in the following proportions: three-quarters teaspoon table salt equals just under one teaspoon Kosher or sea salt.
thyme

Mushrooms, dried
Italian *porcini*, also sold under their French name, *cèpes*. Stored airtight in a cool place, they will keep up to a year.

Nuts, whole, chopped or slivered
pine nuts (pignoli)
walnuts

Oils
corn, safflower, or vegetable
Because these neutral-tasting oils have high smoking points, they are good for high-heat sautéing.
olive oil
Olive oil ranges in color from pale yellow to dark green and in taste from mild and delicate to rich and fruity. Different olive oils can be used for different purposes: for example, stronger ones for cooking, lighter ones for salads. The finest quality olive oil is labeled extra-virgin or virgin.
walnut oil
Rich and nutty tasting. It turns rancid easily, so keep it in a tightly closed container in the refrigerator.

Olives
Kalamata olives
oil-cured black olives

Onions
Store all dry-skinned onions in a cool, dry, well-ventilated place.
red or Italian onions
Zesty tasting and generally eaten raw. The perfect salad onion.
shallots
The most subtle member of the onion family, the shallot has a delicate garlic flavor.
yellow onions
All-purpose cooking onions, strong in taste.

Pasta
angel hair (*capelli d'angelo*)
fedelini
fettuccine
linguine, white and green
pappardelle
penne
spaghettini

Peppers
Bottled Italian pickled peppers are available sweet, medium hot, and hot.

Potatoes, boiling and baking
"New" potatoes are not a particular kind of potato,

but any potato that has not been stored.

Rice

Arborio

This pearly, round-grain rice, imported from Italy, is preferred for *risotto*.

long-grain white rice

Slender grains, much longer than they are wide, that become light and fluffy when cooked and are best for general use.

Stock, chicken and beef

For maximum flavor and quality, your own stock is best (see recipe page 13), but canned stock, or broth, is adequate for most recipes and convenient to have.

Sugar

granulated sugar

Tomatoes

Italian plum tomatoes

Canned plum tomatoes (preferably imported) are an acceptable substitute for fresh.

tomato paste

Sometimes available in tubes, which can be refrigerated and kept for future use after a small amount is gone. With canned paste, spoon out unused portions in one-tablespoon amounts onto waxed paper and freeze, then lift the frozen paste off and store in a plastic container.

Vinegars

balsamic vinegar

Aged vinegar with a complex sweet and sour taste

red and white wine vinegars

tarragon vinegar

A white wine vinegar flavored with fresh tarragon, it is especially good in salads.

Wines and spirits

Marsala, sweet and dry
sherry, dry
red wine, dry
vermouth, dry
white wine, dry

IN THE REFRIGERATOR:

Basil

Though fresh basil is widely available only in summer, try to use it whenever possible to replace dried; the flavor is markedly superior. Stand the stems, preferably with roots intact, in a jar of water, and loosely cover leaves with a plastic bag.

Bread crumbs

You need never buy bread crumbs. To make fresh crumbs, use fresh or day-old bread and process in food processor or blender. For dried, toast bread 30 minutes in preheated 250-degree oven, turning occasionally to prevent slices from browning. Proceed as for fresh. Store bread crumbs in an airtight container: fresh crumbs in the refrigerator, and dried crumbs in a cool, dry place. Either type may also be frozen for several weeks if tightly wrapped in a plastic bag.

Butter

Many cooks prefer unsalted butter because of its finer flavor and because it does not burn as easily as salted.

Cheese

Asiago

A firm, pale-yellow cheese with tiny holes, Asiago is a good table cheese when young, and an excellent sharp grating cheese when aged.

Fontina

A mild cheese resembling Swiss, it is prized for its excellent melting qualities.

Mozzarella

This favorite pizza cheese is bland and semi-firm in its packaged form; freshly made mozzarella is moister and more delicate. Both melt superbly.

Parmesan

Italy's best known grating cheese, it should be bought by the piece and grated as needed; the pre-grated, packaged variety is tasteless by comparison. The finest imported Parmesan is labeled Parmigiano-Reggiano.

Romano

Also a popular grating cheese, Romano is stronger and saltier than Parmesan. Pecorino Romano is the sheep's-milk version of this cheese.

Chives

Refrigerate fresh chives wrapped in plastic. You may also buy small pots of growing chives—keep them on a windowsill and snip as needed.

Cream

heavy cream

Eggs

Will keep 4 to 5 weeks in refrigerator. For best results, bring to room temperature before using.

Lemons

In addition to its many uses in cooking, a slice of lemon rubbed over cut apples and pears will keep them from discoloring. Do not substitute bottled juice or lemon extract.

Milk

Mint

Fresh mint will keep for a week if wrapped in a damp paper towel and enclosed in a plastic bag.

Parsley

The two most commonly available kinds of parsley are flat-leaved and curly; they can be used interchangeably when necessary. Flat-leaved parsley has a more distinctive flavor and is generally preferred in cooking. Curly parsley wilts less easily and is excellent for garnishing. Store parsley in a glass of water and cover loosely with a plastic bag. It will keep for a week in the refrigerator. Or wash and dry it, and refrigerate in a small plastic bag with a dry paper towel inside to absorb any moisture.

Scallions

Scallions have a mild onion flavor. Store wrapped in plastic.

Yeast, active dry

Equipment

Proper cooking equipment makes the work light and is a good cook's most prized possession. You can cook expertly without a store-bought steamer or even a food processor, but basic pans, knives, and a few other items are indispensable. Below are the things you need—and some attractive options—for preparing the menus in this volume.

Pots and pans

Large kettle or stockpot with cover
3 skillets (large, medium, small) with covers; one nonaluminum
2 heavy-gauge sauté pans, 10 to 12 inches in diameter, with covers and ovenproof handles
3 saucepans with covers (1-, 2-, and 4-quart capacities)
 Choose heavy-gauge enameled cast-iron, plain cast-iron, aluminum-clad stainless steel, and aluminum (but you need at least one saucepan that is not aluminum). Best—but very expensive—is tin-lined copper.

Large, heavy-gauge roasting pan
Broiler pan with rack
Shallow baking pan (13 x 9 x 2-inch)
2 cookie sheets (11 x 17-inch)
15-inch round pizza pan
Large flameproof casserole with tight-fitting cover
Flameproof glass baking dish
Heatproof serving bowl
2 heatproof serving platters
Four 4-ounce ramekins or small custard cups
9-inch pie plate
Salad bowl

Knives

A carbon-steel knife takes a sharp edge but tends to rust. You must wash and dry it after each use; otherwise it can blacken foods and counter tops. Good-quality stainless-steel knives, frequently honed, are less trouble and will serve just as well in the home kitchen. Never put a fine knife in the dishwasher. Rinse it, dry it, and put it away—but not loose in a drawer. Knives will stay sharp and last a long time if they have their own storage rack.

Small paring knife
10-inch chef's knife
Bread knife (serrated blade)
Sharpening steel

Other cooking tools

2 sets of mixing bowls in graduated sizes
Colander, with a round base (stainless steel, aluminum, or enamel)
2 strainers in fine and coarse mesh
2 sets of measuring cups and spoons in graduated sizes
 One for dry ingredients, another for shortenings and liquids.
Cooking spoon
Slotted spoon
Long-handled wooden spoons
Wooden spatula (for stirring hot ingredients)
2 metal spatulas or turners (for lifting hot foods from pans)
Slotted spatula

Rubber or vinyl spatula (for folding in ingredients)
Rolling pin
Grater (metal, with several sizes of holes)
 A rotary grater is handy for hard cheese.
2 wire whisks
Pair of metal tongs
Wooden board
Vegetable steamer
Garlic press
Vegetable peeler
Mortar and pestle
Ladle
Pastry brush for basting (a small, new paintbrush that is not nylon serves well)
Cooling rack
Kitchen shears
Kitchen timer
Aluminum foil
Paper towels
Plastic wrap
Waxed paper
Thin rubber gloves

Electric appliances

Food processor or blender
 A blender will do most of the work required in this volume, but a food processor will do it more quickly and in larger volume. A food processor should be considered a necessity, not a luxury, for anyone who enjoys cooking.
Electric mixer

Optional cooking tools

Salad spinner
Food mill
Mandoline
Salad servers
Citrus juicer
 Inexpensive glass kind from the dime store will do.
Nutmeg grater
Kitchen mallet
Flametamer or asbestos mat
Instant-reading meat thermometer
Zester
Pizza wheel
Roll of masking tape or white paper tape for labeling and dating

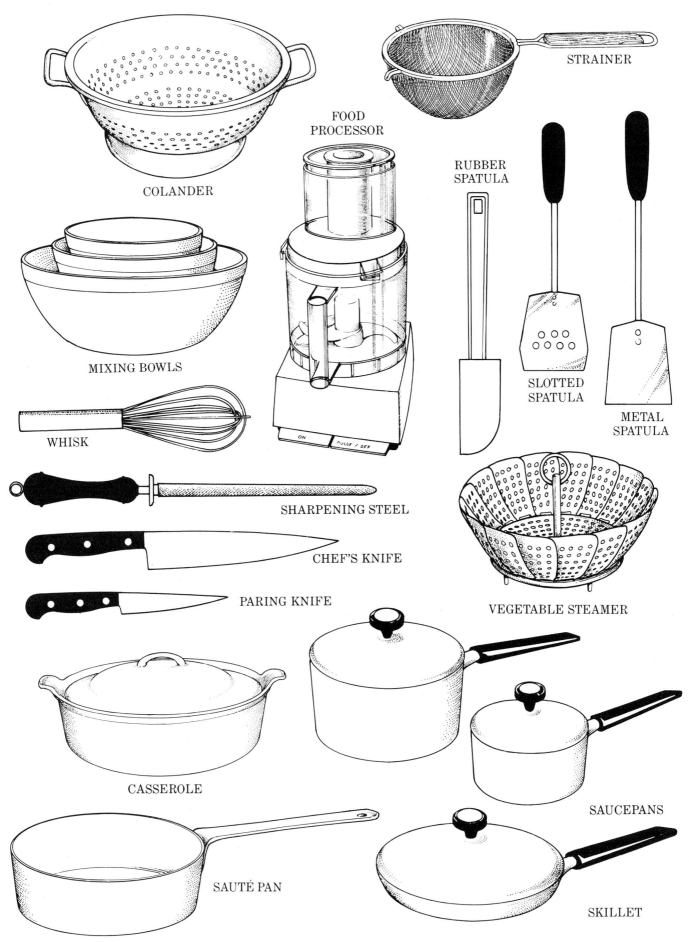

COLANDER

STRAINER

FOOD
PROCESSOR

RUBBER
SPATULA

MIXING BOWLS

SLOTTED
SPATULA

METAL
SPATULA

WHISK

ON   PULSE / OFF

SHARPENING STEEL

CHEF'S KNIFE

PARING KNIFE

VEGETABLE STEAMER

CASSEROLE

SAUCEPANS

SAUTÉ PAN

SKILLET

17

Silvana La Rocca

B orn into an Italian family that subscribes to the ancient saying *la civiltà sta nel piatto* (civilization can be found on a plate), Silvana La Rocca was exposed to good cooking and fine dining at an early age. Her maternal grandmother taught her how to make fresh pasta; her mother introduced her to the vast diversity of Italian cooking; and her father taught her how to select the freshest ingredients at the market and to prepare them simply in the Abruzzo style.

Still an adherent of Abruzzese cooking, Silvana La Rocca offers three meals featuring dishes and ingredients popular in that region. In Menus 1 and 2 she flavors the entrées, chicken and sole, respectively, with olive oil, garlic, and black pepper—all typical Abruzzese seasonings. She adds white wine and rosemary to the chicken and heightens the flavor of the tomato sauce for the sole with capers. The fish recipe is named for her grandmother.

In Menu 3 she features lamb chops that in Italy are called *agnello brucialingua*, or "lamb that burns the tongue," because they are fried with hot chili peppers. According to the cook, the accompanying potatoes (potato wedges baked in their skins with onions and carrots) are often prepared by Abruzzese hunters on trips to the mountains. The green bean and mint salad is a refreshing counterpoint to the spicy lamb.

Fresh flowers and a richly patterned cloth set a festive tone for this colorful dinner. Golden-brown chicken pieces tossed with strips of red pepper are the appetizing entrée. Serve the cheese-and-herb-filled porcini *mushroom caps and the radicchio and mozzarella salad in separate pottery dishes.*

18

Stuffed Porcini Mushrooms
Chicken with Peppers
Radicchio and Mozzarella Salad

Large-capped meaty *funghi porcini*, called pigs' mushrooms because pigs love their flavor, are prized in Italy as a delicacy. Because *porcini* have a short growing season and are highly perishable, fresh ones may be difficult to locate at a greengrocer or an Italian market. As a substitute, use very large white cultivated mushrooms. Buy mushrooms that are fresh looking, unblemished, and have tightly fitting caps with no gills showing. Mushrooms will keep briefly in the refrigerator in a bowl covered with a damp towel, but they are best used the same day they are bought. Never wash or soak mushrooms; they absorb water and lose their flavor. Simply wipe them clean with a damp paper towel.

WHAT TO DRINK

Choose a full-bodied, very dry white wine such as an Italian Greco di Tufo or Pinot Bianco, or a California Pinot Blanc, for this northern Italian menu.

SHOPPING LIST AND STAPLES

2½ to 3 pounds chicken parts
2 to 3 heads radicchio (about ¾ pound total weight)
2 medium-size red bell peppers (about ½ pound total weight)
4 large fresh porcini mushrooms, or 4 extra-large cultivated mushrooms (about ¼ pound total weight)
4 cloves garlic
Small bunch fresh parsley
Small bunch fresh mint, or ½ teaspoon dried
Small bunch fresh basil, or 1 tablespoon dried
Small bunch fresh rosemary, or 1½ tablespoons dried
2 large lemons
½ pound fresh mozzarella or good-quality packaged mozzarella or Monterey Jack
2 ounces Parmesan cheese, preferably imported
1 cup olive oil, approximately
2-ounce tin flat oil-packed anchovy fillets
1 cup all-purpose flour
Salt and freshly ground black pepper
½ cup dry white wine or dry vermouth

UTENSILS

Food processor or blender
Large heavy-gauge nonaluminum skillet
Large heavy-gauge nonaluminum roasting pan
Small shallow baking dish
9-inch pie pan or plate
Small bowl
Measuring cups and spoons
Chef's knife
Paring knife
2 wooden spoons
Large metal spoon
Rubber spatula
Grater (if not using processor)
Metal tongs

START-TO-FINISH STEPS

1. Squeeze lemon juice for mushrooms and salad recipes. Wash parsley and fresh herbs, if using, dry with paper towels, and set aside. Peel garlic for chicken and mushrooms recipes.
2. Follow salad recipe steps 1 through 3.
3. Follow mushrooms recipe steps 1 through 7.
4. Follow chicken recipe steps 1 through 5.
5. While chicken is browning, follow mushrooms recipe step 8 and salad recipe step 4.
6. Follow chicken recipe steps 6 through 8.
7. While chicken bakes, follow mushrooms recipe step 9 and serve as appetizer.
8. Follow salad recipe step 5, chicken recipe step 9, and serve.

RECIPES

Stuffed Porcini Mushrooms

4 large fresh porcini mushrooms, or 4 extra-large cultivated mushrooms (about ¼ pound total weight)
Small bunch fresh parsley
2 ounces Parmesan cheese, preferably imported
2-ounce tin flat oil-packed anchovy fillets
1 clove garlic, peeled
4 fresh basil leaves, or 1 tablespoon dried
2 tablespoons lemon juice
1 teaspoon freshly ground black pepper
¼ cup olive oil

1. Preheat oven to 375 degrees.
2. Wipe mushrooms with damp cloth or paper towel. Carefully remove stems and reserve. Place mushrooms cap-side down in small baking dish; set aside.

3. Remove stems from parsley, and coarsely chop enough sprigs to measure ¼ cup. Reserve remaining sprigs for garnish, if desired.
4. Using food processor or grater, grate enough Parmesan to measure ¼ cup.
5. Drain 4 anchovy fillets and set aside; reserve oil and remaining fillets for another use.
6. In food processor or blender, combine mushroom stems, garlic, basil, anchovy fillets, Parmesan, lemon juice, parsley, and black pepper. Process 45 seconds. Scrape down sides of bowl and process another 30 seconds, or until mixture is medium-coarse.
7. Divide filling among mushroom caps, spoon 1 tablespoon olive oil over each mushroom, and set aside.
8. Place mushrooms in oven and bake 12 to 15 minutes, or until filling shrinks away slightly from sides of caps.
9. Transfer mushrooms to serving dish and garnish with parsley, if desired.

Chicken with Peppers

2½ to 3 pounds chicken parts
1 cup all-purpose flour
Salt
2 sprigs fresh rosemary, or 1½ tablespoons dried
⅓ cup olive oil
2 to 3 cloves garlic, peeled
2 medium-size red bell peppers (about ½ pound total weight)
½ cup dry white wine or dry vermouth
Freshly ground black pepper

1. Rinse chicken under cold running water and dry thoroughly with paper towels. Place flour in pie pan or plate. Sprinkle chicken with salt and lightly dredge each piece in flour, coating evenly; shake off excess and set aside. Chop rosemary sprigs and set aside.
2. In large heavy-gauge skillet, heat olive oil over medium-high heat. Add garlic and sauté, stirring occasionally, 2 to 3 minutes, or until golden brown.
3. Remove garlic and discard. Place chicken in skillet in single layer, skin side down, increase heat to high, and sauté until one side is golden brown, 3 to 4 minutes.
4. While chicken is browning, halve, core, and seed bell peppers. Cut into ¼-inch-thick strips and set aside.
5. Turn chicken with tongs and sauté other side until evenly browned, 3 to 4 minutes. Meanwhile, lightly oil roasting pan.
6. Remove skillet from heat and transfer chicken pieces to roasting pan. Pour off fat from skillet, leaving about 2 tablespoons, and return skillet to medium heat. Add wine, increase heat to medium-high, and boil 1 to 2 minutes, or until liquid is reduced by half.
7. Lower heat to medium, add bell pepper strips and rosemary, and cook, stirring, another 2 minutes.
8. Spoon bell pepper mixture over chicken pieces, sprinkle with freshly ground black pepper to taste, and bake, uncovered, in preheated 375-degree oven 15 minutes.
9. Transfer chicken and peppers to platter and serve.

Radicchio and Mozzarella Salad

2 to 3 heads radicchio (about ¾ pound total weight)
½ pound fresh mozzarella, or good-quality packaged mozzarella or Monterey Jack
7 fresh mint leaves, or ½ teaspoon dried
2 to 3 tablespoons lemon juice
⅓ cup olive oil
Salt and freshly ground black pepper

1. Wash radicchio and discard any bruised or wilted leaves. Dry with paper towels and place in salad bowl.
2. Cut cheese into thin 1½-inch-long strips and place on top of radicchio.
3. If using fresh mint, tear leaves into small pieces and sprinkle over salad. (If using dried, do not add at this point.) Cover bowl with plastic wrap and refrigerate until ready to serve.
4. In small bowl, combine lemon juice, olive oil, and dried mint, if using. Add salt and pepper to taste and, with fork, stir dressing until blended; set aside.
5. Just before serving, stir dressing to recombine, add to salad, and toss gently.

ADDED TOUCH

For this dessert, select fresh figs that are medium-soft and that exude a drop of liquid from the rounded blossom end.

Fresh Figs in Monks' Robes

8 large fresh figs with smooth skins (about 1½ pounds total weight)
8 blanched almonds
¾ cup unsweetened cocoa powder
¾ cup confectioners' sugar

1. Peel each fig carefully: Holding fig pointed end down, make shallow crosswise incision with paring knife just beneath skin at rounded end. Holding skin firmly against blade with your thumb, run knife underneath skin while gently pulling downward in the same motion. Repeat until all skin is removed.

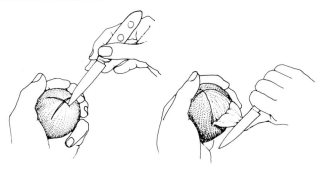

2. Press a whole blanched almond into bottom end of each fig until totally enclosed.
3. Sift cocoa and sugar together into shallow dish.
4. Roll each fig in cocoa-sugar mixture until evenly coated.
5. Place figs on small platter, cover, and refrigerate for 15 to 20 minutes before serving.

Fillets of Sole Signora Concetta
Baked Onions
Fresh Tomato Salad

Sole fillets and crescents of baked onion look dramatic against solid black plates. The tomato salad adds extra color.

Special brine-cured olives garnish the sole fillets. The cook suggests using either tiny Italian Gaeta olives or Niçoise olives from France, which range in color from brown to purple to black.

WHAT TO DRINK

The fresh, lively flavors of these dishes suggest a crisp, dry white wine as an accompaniment. A Verdicchio or Pinot Grigio would do very well, as would a California Sauvignon Blanc.

SHOPPING LIST AND STAPLES

4 medium-size fillets of sole (about 1¾ pounds total weight)
4 large tomatoes (about 3 pounds total weight)
Extra-large onion (about 1½ pounds)

Small bunch scallions
2 cloves garlic
Small bunch fresh parsley
Small bunch fresh basil, or 2 teaspoons dried
Large lemon
16-ounce can imported plum tomatoes
¼ pound Parmesan cheese, preferably imported
1¼ cups olive oil
2 tablespoons white wine vinegar
2-ounce jar imported capers
7-ounce jar small dark olives, preferably Gaeta or Niçoise
¾ cup all-purpose flour
1 tablespoon sugar
2 teaspoons fennel seeds
1 teaspoon dried oregano
Salt
Freshly ground black pepper
Freshly ground white pepper
½ cup dry white wine or dry vermouth

22

Large heavy-gauge nonaluminum skillet
Medium-size nonaluminum skillet
Large saucepan
Medium-size nonaluminum baking dish
Large bowl
Medium-size bowl
Colander
Large strainer
Measuring cups and spoons
Chef's knife
Paring knife
Wooden spoon
Wide metal spatula
Rubber spatula
Zester
Grater

START-TO-FINISH STEPS

1. Follow onions recipe steps 1 and 2.
2. Follow sole recipe steps 1 and 2.
3. Follow onions recipe step 3.
4. While onion is cooking, follow salad recipe step 1.
5. Follow onions recipe step 4.
6. Follow sole recipe steps 3 and 4.
7. Follow onions recipe steps 5 and 6.
8. While onions bake, follow salad recipe step 2.
9. Follow sole recipe steps 5 through 9.
10. While sauce for sole is being reheated, follow onions recipe step 7 and salad recipe steps 3 and 4.
11. Follow sole recipe step 10, onions recipe step 8, and serve with salad.

RECIPES

Fillets of Sole Signora Concetta

2 cloves garlic, peeled and chopped
Small bunch fresh basil, or 2 teaspoons dried
16-ounce can imported plum tomatoes, drained
2 tablespoons imported capers
½ cup olive oil
½ cup dry white wine or dry vermouth
Salt and freshly ground black pepper
4 medium-size fillets of sole
¾ cup all-purpose flour
¼ pound Parmesan cheese, preferably imported
½ cup small dark olives, preferably Gaeta or Niçoise

1. If using fresh basil, rinse and pat dry. Reserve 5 or 6 leaves and refrigerate remainder for another use.
2. Coarsely chop enough tomatoes to measure 1½ cups, reserving remainder for another use. Drain capers.
3. In medium-size nonaluminum skillet, heat ¼ cup olive oil over medium-high heat. Add garlic and sauté 2 to 3 minutes, or until golden.
4. Add tomatoes, basil, capers, and wine to skillet, and stir to combine. Raise heat to high and quickly bring sauce

to a boil. Remove skillet from heat immediately, add salt and pepper to taste, and set aside.
5. Rinse fillets under cold water and dry with paper towels. Place flour on sheet of waxed paper. Sprinkle both sides of fillets with salt and pepper. Dredge fillets in flour, making sure each piece is well coated; shake off excess.
6. In large heavy-gauge nonaluminum skillet, heat remaining ¼ cup olive oil over medium-high heat. When oil is hot, add fillets, arranging in single layer, and lightly brown on one side, about 4 minutes.
7. Meanwhile, grate enough Parmesan to measure ⅓ cup. Remove pits from olives; set aside.
8. Turn fish and brown another 4 minutes.
9. Return sauce to medium heat and warm 2 to 3 minutes.
10. Divide fish among dinner plates. Top each fillet with hot tomato sauce, sprinkle with freshly grated Parmesan, and garnish with black olives.

Baked Onions

Extra-large onion (about 1½ pounds)
1 tablespoon sugar
2 teaspoons fennel seeds
Salt and freshly ground white pepper
¼ cup olive oil
2 tablespoons white wine vinegar

1. Preheat oven to 400 degrees.
2. In large saucepan, bring 2 quarts water to a boil over high heat.
3. Cut off root end of onion and peel. Plunge onion into boiling water and boil 5 minutes.
4. Transfer onion to colander, drain, and set aside to cool.
5. Peel and quarter onion; cut quarters into thirds and arrange in single layer in baking dish. Sprinkle with sugar, fennel seeds, and salt and pepper to taste. Drizzle with olive oil and toss onions until coated.
6. Bake 30 to 35 minutes, or until onions are light golden.
7. Remove from oven and allow to cool 5 to 6 minutes.
8. Sprinkle onions with vinegar and divide among plates.

Fresh Tomato Salad

4 large tomatoes (about 3 pounds total weight), washed
4 scallions, washed, trimmed, and chopped
5 sprigs parsley, washed and chopped
Large lemon, washed
1 teaspoon dried oregano
Salt and freshly ground black pepper
½ cup olive oil

1. Cut tomatoes into eighths or narrow wedges and place in large bowl. Add scallions and parsley to tomatoes.
2. Holding lemon over bowl with tomatoes, remove zest, allowing it to fall into bowl.
3. Cut lemon in half and squeeze enough juice to measure 3 tablespoons; add to tomatoes.
4. Season tomatoes with oregano and salt and pepper to taste, drizzle with olive oil, and toss gently. Adjust seasoning, toss again, and divide among individual salad plates.

Spicy Lamb Chops
Hunter-style Potatoes
Green Beans with Mint

Serve each of your guests a lamb chop garnished with a chili pepper and sage, some roasted vegetables, and a bean salad.

For the lamb recipe, use fresh hot chilies such as *jalapeños* or *serranos*. Take special care when handling chilies; they contain a highly irritating substance that can burn the skin or cause a rash. Wear thin rubber gloves while working with chilies. After removing the gloves, do not touch your face until you have thoroughly washed your hands with soap and warm water.

WHAT TO DRINK

You will need a sturdy red wine to stand up to the lamb. A Chianti Classico Riserva would be ideal, or try an Italian Taurasi or a California Cabernet Sauvignon.

SHOPPING LIST AND STAPLES

Four 1¼-inch-thick loin lamb chops (about 1½ pounds total weight)
1 pound green beans
4 medium-size boiling potatoes (about 1½ pounds total weight)
2 medium-size yellow onions (about 1 pound total weight)
4 medium-size carrots (about 1 pound total weight)
4 fresh hot chili peppers, or 1½ to 3 tablespoons red pepper flakes
1 head garlic
Small bunch fresh mint leaves, or 1 teaspoon dried

Small bunch fresh sage, or ½ teaspoon dried
1 lemon
1¼ cups olive oil, approximately
2 tablespoons white wine vinegar
1 tablespoon dried rosemary
Salt
Freshly ground black pepper
Freshly ground white pepper
½ cup dry white wine or dry vermouth

UTENSILS

Stockpot or large kettle
Large heavy-gauge nonaluminum skillet
13 x 9 x 2-inch nonaluminum baking dish
Colander
Measuring cups and spoons
Chef's knife
Paring knife
2 wooden spoons
Slotted metal spoon
Metal spatula
Metal tongs
Vegetable peeler

START-TO-FINISH STEPS

1. Prepare fresh herbs, if using.
2. Follow potatoes recipe steps 1 and 2.
3. Follow green beans recipe steps 1 through 3.
4. Follow potatoes recipe steps 3 and 4.
5. Follow green beans recipe step 4 and lamb recipe steps 1 through 5.
6. Follow potatoes recipe step 5 and green beans recipe steps 5 and 6.
7. Follow lamb recipe step 6.
8. Follow potatoes recipe step 6, lamb recipe step 7, and serve with green beans.

RECIPES

Spicy Lamb Chops

4 fresh hot chili peppers, or 1½ to 3 tablespoons red pepper flakes
2 to 4 cloves garlic, peeled
½ cup olive oil
Four 1¼-inch-thick loin lamb chops (about 1½ pounds total weight)
6 to 8 fresh sage leaves, chopped, or ½ teaspoon dried
2 tablespoons white wine vinegar
Salt and freshly ground black pepper
½ cup dry white wine or dry vermouth

1. If using fresh chili peppers, rinse under cold running water and dry with paper towels. Wearing rubber gloves, halve peppers lengthwise, remove seeds, and discard.
2. In large heavy-gauge skillet, heat olive oil over medium-high heat. Add chili peppers and garlic, and sauté 2 to 3 minutes, or until garlic is golden. Discard garlic.

3. Add lamb chops to skillet with chili peppers and brown over medium-high heat 3 to 4 minutes on one side.
4. Turn chops and brown another 3 to 4 minutes.
5. Add sage, vinegar, and salt and pepper to taste. Lower heat to medium, turn chops, and cook, uncovered, 8 minutes for rare, 10 for medium, or 12 for well done.
6. Add wine, raise heat to high, and cook chops another 3 to 5 minutes, or until most of wine has evaporated.
7. Divide chops among dinner plates, top each with a spoonful of pan juice, and serve.

Hunter-style Potatoes

4 medium-size boiling potatoes (about 1½ pounds total weight)
4 medium-size carrots (about 1 pound total weight)
2 medium-size yellow onions (about 1 pound total weight)
8 cloves garlic
1 tablespoon dried rosemary
Salt and freshly ground black pepper
¼ cup olive oil

1. Preheat oven to 400 degrees.
2. Wash and dry potatoes; cut into 1-inch-thick wedges. Trim and peel carrots. Halve carrots lengthwise, then cut into 1-inch-long sticks. Peel and quarter onions.
3. Combine vegetables in baking dish. Add whole, unpeeled garlic cloves, rosemary, and salt and pepper to taste. Drizzle vegetables with olive oil and toss until well coated.
4. Roast vegetables in upper third of oven 15 minutes.
5. Remove dish from oven, turn vegetables, and return dish to oven. Roast another 15 minutes, or until potatoes are tender when pricked with a sharp knife.
6. Divide vegetables among dinner plates.

Green Beans with Mint

Salt
1 pound green beans
1 lemon
10 to 12 fresh mint leaves, shredded, or 1 teaspoon dried
Freshly ground white pepper
¼ to ½ cup olive oil

1. In stockpot or large kettle, bring 4 to 5 quarts of water and 1 tablespoon salt to a boil over high heat.
2. Meanwhile, snap off ends of beans and discard. Wash beans in cold running water and set aside. Squeeze enough lemon to measure about 3 tablespoons juice.
3. Add beans all at once to boiling water. When water returns to a boil, lower heat to medium-high and cook, uncovered, 7 minutes, or until beans are crisp-tender.
4. Turn beans into colander and refresh under cold running water. Drain and set aside until cool.
5. Dry beans thoroughly with paper towels and transfer to serving bowl. Add dried mint, if using, and white pepper to taste. Toss beans with olive oil until thoroughly coated. Add lemon juice, adjust seasoning, and toss again.
6. Add fresh mint, if using, and divide beans among individual salad plates.

Felice and Lidia Bastianich

C ooking comes naturally to Felice and Lidia Bastianich. As a youth he worked at his father's small northern Italian inn, and from the age of 14, she cooked for her entire family. Advocates of using only top-quality ingredients, the Bastianiches plan meals—both at home and in their restaurant— around what is best in the marketplace, then fill in with their own homemade prosciutto and pasta. By adhering to the unpretentious cooking traditions of their native Istria, the Bastianiches serve meals that are simple and nourishing. As Lidia Bastianich says, "We want our customers and guests to be able to duplicate our recipes, so we stick to uncomplicated foods and methods."

Istrian simplicity underlies each of the menus they present here. The sautéed shrimp of Menu 1 are lightly seasoned with garlic, lemon juice, and white wine, and are served on a bed of risotto. The asparagus spears are broiled with a light coating of melted butter and grated Parmesan.

In Istria, where game is abundant, cooks often serve polenta with wild fowl. Menu 2 offers quail in a tomato sauce flavored with bay leaves, rosemary, and cloves, presented on a platter with polenta. A green bean and bacon salad adds color and texture to this cold-weather meal.

Chicken is the entrée for Menu 3. The breasts are dredged with flour, dipped in parsley and grated Parmesan, and then sautéed in stock with wine and lemon juice. A substantial dish of Swiss chard and potatoes complements the fowl.

A heaping platter of risotto topped with whole shrimp in a garlic and parsley sauce is a delightful entrée for an informal spring dinner. The crisp-tender asparagus spears should be served on a warmed platter.

27

Scampi with Quick Risotto
Asparagus Gratinati

When buying raw shrimp, select those that are plump and odor-free; avoid any with meat that has shrunk away from the shell, which indicates that the shrimp have been frozen and thawed. If the shrimp do not have the shells and veins removed, follow step 1 of the recipe. Because they are highly perishable, shrimp should be purchased at the last minute. If you must store them, do so in a covered container in the coldest part of the refrigerator. After cooking, the shrimp should be firm and crisp.

WHAT TO DRINK

A well-chilled fruity white wine such as an Italian Chardonnay or Vernaccia, or a California Sauvignon Blanc or Riesling, goes well with the scampi.

SHOPPING LIST AND STAPLES

24 large shrimp (about 1¼ pounds total weight)
16 medium-size asparagus spears (about 1 pound total weight)
Medium-size yellow onion
4 cloves garlic
Small bunch parsley
1 lemon
3 to 4 cups chicken stock, preferably homemade (see page 13), or canned
1 stick plus 2 tablespoons unsalted butter
6 ounces Parmesan cheese, preferably imported
¼ cup plus 2 tablespoons olive oil
2 cups long-grain rice
3 tablespoons dry bread crumbs
Salt and freshly ground black pepper
½ cup dry white wine

UTENSILS

Food processor (optional)
Stockpot or large saucepan with cover
Large heavy-gauge skillet
Large heavy-gauge saucepan with cover
Small heavy-gauge saucepan or butter warmer
13 x 9-inch flameproof baking dish
Large serving platter
Colander
Measuring cups and spoons
Chef's knife
Paring knife
2 wooden spoons
Metal tongs
Grater (if not using processor)
Juicer
Kitchen string

START-TO-FINISH STEPS

1. Grate enough Parmesan to measure 1 cup for risotto recipe and ½ cup for asparagus recipe.
2. Follow scampi recipe steps 1 and 2.
3. Follow asparagus recipe steps 1 through 3 and scampi recipe step 3.
4. Follow asparagus recipe step 4 and risotto recipe steps 1 through 3.
5. Follow asparagus recipe steps 5 through 7.
6. Follow risotto recipe steps 4 and 5, and scampi recipe steps 4 through 6.
7. Follow asparagus recipe step 8 and scampi recipe step 7.
8. Follow risotto recipe step 6, scampi recipe step 8, and serve with asparagus.

RECIPES

Scampi with Quick Risotto

24 large shrimp (about 1¼ pounds total weight)
4 cloves garlic
Small bunch parsley
1 lemon
¼ cup olive oil
4 tablespoons unsalted butter
½ cup dry white wine
Salt and freshly ground black pepper
3 tablespoons dry bread crumbs
Quick Risotto (see following recipe)

1. Pinch off legs of shrimp, several at a time, then bend back and snap off sharp, beaklike pieces of shell just above tail. Remove shell and discard. Using sharp paring knife, make shallow incision along back of each shrimp, exposing digestive vein. Extract vein and discard (see illustration on next page).
2. Place shrimp in colander, rinse under cold running water, drain, and dry with paper towels. Set aside.
3. Peel and finely chop garlic. Rinse parsley, dry, and chop enough to measure 3 tablespoons. Squeeze enough lemon juice to measure 2 teaspoons; set aside.
4. In large heavy-gauge skillet, heat olive oil over

medium-high heat. Add shrimp and sauté, stirring, about 2 minutes, or until slightly golden.

5. Stir in garlic and sauté 3 minutes, or until golden.

6. Add butter, lemon juice, white wine, and salt and pepper to taste, and cook about 5 minutes, or until shrimp begin to curl and turn opaque.

7. Sprinkle shrimp with parsley and bread crumbs, and cook another minute.

8. Turn shrimp and sauce onto platter with risotto.

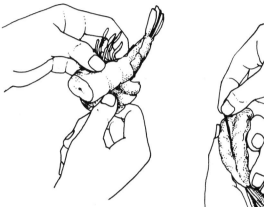

Pinch off legs to remove shell.

Extract digestive vein with your fingers.

Quick Risotto

Medium-size yellow onion
2 tablespoons olive oil
2 cups long-grain rice
4 tablespoons unsalted butter
3 to 4 cups chicken stock
Salt and freshly ground black pepper
1 cup freshly grated Parmesan cheese

1. Peel and chop onion.

2. In large heavy-gauge saucepan, heat oil over medium-high heat. Add onion and sauté 5 minutes, or until golden.

3. Stir in rice, butter, 3 cups chicken stock, and salt and pepper to taste. Reduce heat to low, cover, and cook, stirring occasionally, 10 minutes. If rice sticks to pan, add small amounts of stock, stirring after each addition until incorporated.

4. After 10 minutes, remove cover and allow excess stock to boil off; or, if rice seems too dry, add small amounts of stock, cover, and continue simmering another 5 to 10 minutes, or until rice is tender and all liquid is absorbed. Keep pan covered until ready to serve.

5. Meanwhile, place serving platter under hot running water to warm.

6. When ready to serve, dry platter. Add Parmesan to rice and stir until combined. Turn out onto warm platter.

Asparagus Gratinati

16 medium-size asparagus spears (about 1 pound total weight)

2 tablespoons unsalted butter
½ cup freshly grated Parmesan cheese

1. In stockpot or large saucepan, bring 1 quart of water to a boil over high heat.

2. Meanwhile, rinse asparagus under cold running water and drain. Trim off woody stems and, if desired, peel.

3. Using kitchen string, tie asparagus into 2 bundles. Stand upright in pot, cover, and cook over high heat 6 minutes, or until crisp-tender.

4. With tongs, transfer bundles to colander, untie, and let cool.

5. In small heavy-gauge saucepan or butter warmer, melt butter over low heat.

6. In flameproof baking dish, arrange asparagus spears side by side in single layer and drizzle with melted butter. Sprinkle with Parmesan and set aside.

7. Preheat broiler.

8. Before serving, broil asparagus about 4 inches from heating element 3 to 5 minutes, or just until cheese turns light golden.

ADDED TOUCH

When you ignite the warmed brandy and Grand Marnier for flambéing the strawberries, the flames may be high at first but should die down quickly. If they do not subside, simply put a cover on the skillet.

Flamed Strawberries

1 pint fresh strawberries
Large orange
½ pint heavy cream
¼ cup sugar
2 tablespoons Grand Marnier or other orange liqueur
2 tablespoons brandy
1 pint vanilla ice cream

1. Place medium-size bowl and beaters in freezer to chill.

2. Rinse strawberries and pat dry with paper towels. With sharp paring knife, hull berries and set aside.

3. Rinse orange and dry. Grate enough rind to measure about 3 tablespoons. Cut orange in half. Squeeze juice from one half, reserving remaining half for another use.

4. Pour heavy cream into chilled bowl and whip with electric mixer at high speed until stiff. Cover and refrigerate.

5. In small heavy-gauge skillet, heat sugar over medium heat, stirring, until melted and golden, about 5 minutes.

6. Stir orange rind into sugar and cook about 2 minutes, or until sugar is light brown and syrupy.

7. Add strawberries, orange juice, Grand Marnier, and brandy, and stir to combine. Simmer gently, turning berries to coat with syrup, another 3 minutes.

8. Remove skillet from heat and, averting your face, ignite syrup. When flames have subsided, set skillet aside.

9. Place a generous spoonful of whipped cream in center of each of 4 dessert plates. Top each with a scoop of ice cream and surround "islands" with strawberries. Spoon remaining syrup over ice cream and serve.

Quail with Polenta
Green Bean, Red Onion, and Bacon Salad

Arrange the sautéed quail attractively around the polenta and garnish with a sprig of parsley, if desired; extra sauce may be served on the side. Bacon and red onion rings add color to the green beans.

A popular game bird considered a delicacy throughout the world, quail has pale-colored flesh that tastes like a gamy version of dark-meat chicken. Fresh quail are now available year-round at many butchers, but can also be ordered through the mail (page 103). When buying quail, select those that are plump and silky-skinned with no discoloration. Small Rock Cornish hens can be substituted for quail. They are larger than quail, so you will need only one hen per serving.

WHAT TO DRINK

For this cold-weather meal, the cooks suggest a full-bodied red Barolo or Barbaresco from the Italian Piedmont or a Merlot from Friuli. California Merlot is a good domestic alternative.

SHOPPING LIST AND STAPLES

8 quail (about 3½ pounds total weight), or 4 small
    Rock Cornish hens (about ¾ pound each)
6 slices bacon
1 pound green beans
2 medium-size yellow onions (about 1 pound total weight)
Small red onion
Small bunch fresh rosemary, or ½ teaspoon dried
3 tablespoons unsalted butter
2 ounces Parmesan cheese (optional)
2 cups chicken stock, preferably homemade
    (see page 13), or canned
6-ounce can tomato paste
1 cup olive or vegetable oil, approximately
3 tablespoons white or red wine vinegar
1 cup imported coarsely ground cornmeal or 1⅓ cups reg-
    ular yellow cornmeal
8 bay leaves, approximately
4 cloves
Salt and freshly ground black pepper
1 cup dry white wine

UTENSILS

Food processor (optional)
Large heavy-gauge skillet
Small skillet
Large heavy-gauge saucepan
Medium-size saucepan with cover

Large heatproof serving platter
Large bowl
Small bowl
Sauceboat or small serving bowl
Colander
Strainer
Rubber spatula
Measuring cups and spoons
Chef's knife
2 wooden spoons
Grater (if not using processor)

START-TO-FINISH STEPS

1. Coarsely chop bacon for quail and salad recipes.
2. Follow salad recipe steps 1 through 3.
3. Follow quail recipe steps 1 and 2.
4. Follow salad recipe step 4 and polenta recipe steps 1 and 2.
5. Follow quail recipe steps 3 through 5.
6. While quail browns, follow salad recipe steps 5 through 8.
7. Follow quail recipe steps 6 and 7.
8. Follow polenta recipe steps 3 through 5, if cooking quail; if cooking hens, wait 10 minutes before beginning polenta recipe step 3, and then proceed through step 5.
9. Follow quail recipe step 8 and serve with polenta and salad.

RECIPES

Quail with Polenta

2 medium-size yellow onions (about 1 pound total weight)
Small bunch fresh rosemary, or ½ teaspoon dried
½ cup olive or vegetable oil
2 slices bacon, coarsely chopped
4 cloves
3 bay leaves
Salt
Freshly ground black pepper
8 quail (about 3½ pounds total weight), or 4 small Rock Cornish hens (about ¾ pound each)
2 ounces Parmesan cheese (optional)
2 teaspoons tomato paste
1 cup dry white wine
2 cups chicken stock
Polenta (see following recipe)

1. Peel and dice onions. Rinse fresh rosemary and pat dry with paper towels. Chop enough to measure 1 teaspoon.
2. In large heavy-gauge skillet, heat oil over medium heat. Add onions, rosemary, bacon, cloves, bay leaves, and salt and pepper to taste, and sauté, stirring occasionally, 5 to 10 minutes, or until onions are nicely browned.
3. Add quail or hens and brown 8 to 10 minutes on one side.
4. If using Parmesan, grate enough in food processor or with grater to measure ¼ cup; set aside.
5. Turn birds and cook another 8 to 10 minutes on other side, or until evenly browned.

6. In small bowl, blend tomato paste and wine. Add mixture to skillet and stir into pan juices until blended, basting birds as you stir. Raise heat to medium-high and simmer until liquid has almost evaporated, about 12 minutes.
7. Add stock and simmer another 15 minutes for quail, or 25 to 30 minutes for hens, or until tip of knife easily penetrates breast and juices run clear.
8. Transfer birds to platter with polenta. Pour sauce through strainer set over sauceboat or small bowl, extruding as much liquid as possible with back of spoon. Spoon sauce over each bird and around polenta. Sprinkle birds with cheese, if using, and serve with remaining sauce.

Polenta

1 cup imported coarsely ground cornmeal or 1⅓ cups regular yellow cornmeal
½ teaspoon salt
3 tablespoons unsalted butter
4 or 5 bay leaves

1. Preheat oven to 200 degrees.
2. In large heavy-gauge saucepan, bring 4 cups water to a boil over high heat.
3. Place serving platter in oven to warm.
4. Reduce heat under saucepan to medium and add cornmeal in a very slow, steady stream, stirring constantly with wooden spoon. Add salt, butter, and bay leaves, and continue stirring until polenta thickens and pulls away from sides of pan, about 15 minutes.
5. Remove bay leaves and discard. With rubber spatula, turn out polenta into middle of warm platter.

Green Bean, Red Onion, and Bacon Salad

1 pound green beans
Small red onion
4 slices bacon, coarsely chopped
3 tablespoons white or red wine vinegar
3 tablespoons olive or vegetable oil, approximately
Salt and freshly ground black pepper

1. In medium-size saucepan, bring 2 quarts of water to a boil over high heat.
2. Meanwhile, trim beans. Peel red onion and cut into thin slices. Separate into rings and set aside.
3. Add beans to boiling water, lower heat to medium, cover, and cook 5 minutes, or just until crisp-tender.
4. Turn beans into colander and refresh under cold running water. Drain and set aside to cool.
5. In small skillet, cook bacon over medium heat, stirring occasionally, 5 minutes, or until crisp.
6. Meanwhile, transfer beans to large bowl.
7. Remove skillet from heat and pour off bacon fat. Add vinegar, stir, and return to heat for 1 minute.
8. Pour bacon and vinegar mixture over beans, add oil and salt and pepper to taste, and toss until combined. Adjust seasoning, toss again, and arrange on serving platter. Top with onion rings and set aside until ready to serve.

Chicken Felice
Swiss Chard and Potatoes

Crisp golden chicken breasts topped with a lemon and wine sauce are accompanied by Swiss chard mashed with potatoes.

The lemony, cheese-encrusted boneless chicken breasts are simple to prepare and are an impressive dinner for company. The vegetable dish of Swiss chard and coarsely mashed potatoes can be varied if you wish: Substitute spinach or savoy cabbage for the chard.

For the best flavor, you should always buy Parmesan cheese by the chunk and grate it at home as needed; a quarter pound produces one cup of grated cheese. Slice off the rind before grating. If you are using a food processor to grate the cheese, cut the cheese into ½-inch cubes before grating with the steel blade.

WHAT TO DRINK

A dry, lightly acidic white Pinot Grigio, Gavi, or Verdicchio would be good here, or choose a domestic Sauvignon Blanc or fully dry Chenin Blanc.

SHOPPING LIST AND STAPLES

4 skinless, boneless chicken breasts (about 1½ pounds total weight), halved and pounded ¼ inch thick

2 bunches Swiss chard (about 4 pounds total weight)
3 medium-size potatoes (about 1¼ pounds total weight)
Small bunch parsley
4 cloves garlic
3 lemons
2½ cups chicken stock, preferably homemade (see page 13), or canned
4 eggs
¼ cup milk
7 tablespoons unsalted butter
2 ounces Parmesan cheese
¼ cup olive oil
½ cup vegetable oil
1 cup all-purpose flour
Salt and freshly ground black pepper
1 cup dry white wine

UTENSILS

Food processor (optional)
Stockpot or large kettle
Large heavy-gauge skillet

Large heavy-gauge saucepan
Large heatproof platter
9-inch pie pan
Large heatproof bowl
Medium-size bowl
Colander
Measuring cups and spoons
Chef's knife
Paring knife
2 wooden spoons
Potato masher
Vegetable peeler (optional)
Metal tongs
Grater (if not using processor)
Juicer

START-TO-FINISH STEPS

1. Follow Swiss chard recipe steps 1 through 4.
2. Follow chicken recipe steps 1 through 3.
3. Follow Swiss chard recipe step 5.
4. Follow chicken recipe steps 4 through 6.
5. Follow Swiss chard recipe step 6.
6. Follow chicken recipe steps 7 through 10.
7. Follow Swiss chard recipe steps 7 through 10.
8. Follow chicken recipe steps 11 and 12 and Swiss chard recipe step 11.
9. Follow chicken recipe steps 13 and 14, and serve with Swiss chard and potatoes.

RECIPES

Chicken Felice

4 tablespoons unsalted butter
Small bunch parsley
2 ounces Parmesan cheese
4 skinless, boneless chicken breasts (about 1½ pounds total weight), halved and pounded ¼ inch thick
4 eggs
¼ cup milk
Salt and freshly ground black pepper
½ cup vegetable oil
1 cup all-purpose flour
3 lemons
1 cup dry white wine
2½ cups chicken stock

1. Preheat oven to 200 degrees. Set out butter to reach room temperature.
2. Wash and dry parsley; chop enough to measure 2 tablespoons and refrigerate remainder for another use. In food processor fitted with steel blade, or with grater, grate enough cheese to measure ½ cup; set aside.
3. Rinse chicken and dry with paper towels.
4. Beat eggs in medium-size bowl. Add milk, grated cheese, chopped parsley, and salt and pepper to taste, and stir to combine.
5. In large heavy-gauge skillet, heat vegetable oil over medium-high heat until hot but not smoking.

6. Place flour in pie pan. One by one, dredge each breast lightly with flour, shake off excess, and dip in egg and cheese mixture, letting excess mixture drip off into bowl. Place coated breasts in skillet and fry 5 minutes on one side, or until golden.
7. Meanwhile, line heatproof platter with double thickness of paper towels. Rinse 2 lemons and dry. Cut each lemon into rounds, then halve, and set aside. Squeeze enough juice from remaining lemon to measure 2 tablespoons.
8. With tongs, turn breasts and fry another 5 minutes on other side, or until golden.
9. Transfer chicken to paper-towel-lined platter, loosely cover with foil, and keep warm in oven.
10. Pour off oil from skillet. Add wine, lemon juice, stock, and salt and pepper to taste to skillet and bring to a boil over medium-high heat. Continue boiling until sauce is reduced to about 1 cup, about 10 to 15 minutes.
11. Place 4 dinner plates in oven to warm.
12. Reduce heat under skillet to medium. Return chicken to skillet and simmer 15 minutes.
13. Transfer chicken to warm plates. Add butter, 1 tablespoon at a time, to liquid in pan, swirling after each addition until butter is incorporated.
14. Remove pan from heat. Top each breast with a generous spoonful of sauce and garnish with lemon slices.

Swiss Chard and Potatoes

2 bunches Swiss chard (about 4 pounds total weight)
3 medium-size potatoes (about 1¼ pounds total weight)
4 cloves garlic
¼ cup olive oil
3 tablespoons unsalted butter
Salt and freshly ground black pepper

1. In stockpot or large kettle, bring 6 quarts of water to a boil over high heat.
2. Meanwhile, trim off lower (stem) half of Swiss chard. Cut leaf tops into 1-inch pieces and wash thoroughly in several changes of cold water to remove all traces of grit.
3. Peel and quarter potatoes.
4. Add potatoes to boiling water and cook 5 minutes.
5. Add Swiss chard to potatoes and cook another 10 minutes.
6. Transfer vegetables to colander and drain.
7. Bruise garlic cloves with flat side of knife blade and peel.
8. In large heavy-gauge saucepan, heat oil over medium heat. Add garlic and sauté, stirring occasionally, until browned, 2 to 3 minutes.
9. Add Swiss chard, potatoes, butter, and salt and pepper to taste, and mash coarsely.
10. Cook mixture, stirring constantly with wooden spoon, 5 minutes.
11. Remove garlic cloves and discard. Turn vegetables into large heatproof bowl and keep warm in 200-degree oven until ready to serve.

Lynne Kasper

L ynne Kasper began her food career studying classic French theory and technique, but has amplified her food knowledge by researching Italian cuisine and history in Europe. Well versed in Italian cooking methods, she nonetheless describes herself as an interpretive cook who likes to vary traditional recipes but still preserve the essence of the originals.

For the risotto of Menu 1, a mainstay of the northern Piedmontese winter diet, she short-cuts the standard lengthy cooking process by covering the risotto while it cooks and stirring it only to prevent sticking. The result is still delicious and creamy.

Menu 2 is in the Renaissance style: The almond broth and broiled leg of lamb both incorporate the sweet, spicy, and savory flavors loved by sixteenth-century cooks. However, Lynne Kasper serves the lamb rare to medium-rare rather than in the traditionally favored well-done style. Roasted potatoes go well with the lamb.

Menu 3, a country-style meal that is good on a chilly fall or winter day, features a first course of prosciutto with *mostarda di Cremona*, a spicy fruit relish imported from Cremona in Lombardy. The main course is a rich minestrone from the Marches region, served with crusty Italian bread.

Serve your guests the refreshing escarole, red onion, and coppa *salad as a first course, and while they are enjoying it, finish preparing the peasant-style risotto.*

Escarole, Onion, and Coppa Salad
Peasant-style Risotto

The light prelude to this substantial meal is a simple salad of escarole, onion, and *coppa* (see page 10 for more information about this Italian meat). A member of the endive family, escarole has a bushy head with broad, slightly curled, dark green leaves. If you plan to store the escarole for several days before using it, leave the head intact, place it in a plastic bag, and store in the refrigerator; wash just before using. You may wish to vary this salad by adding chopped bell peppers, marinated mushrooms, and quartered artichoke hearts. To dress the salad, the cook suggests a flavorful extra-virgin olive oil, particularly one from Tuscany or Liguria.

WHAT TO DRINK

The hearty main dish needs a medium-bodied red wine with a good flavor. The cook likes Barbera d'Alba, but a Barbera d'Asti, a Dolcetto, or a California Zinfandel is also fine.

SHOPPING LIST AND STAPLES

1¼ pounds mild home-style Italian sausage
2 ounces sliced sweet coppa or capocollo
1 ounce sliced hot coppa or capocollo
Small head cabbage (about 1 pound)
2 medium-size yellow onions (about 1 pound total weight)
Medium-size red onion
2 medium-size carrots (about ¾ pound total weight)
Medium-size head escarole
Small bunch fresh basil, or ½ teaspoon dried, approximately
Small bunch fresh marjoram, or ½ teaspoon dried
Small bunch fresh rosemary, or ½ teaspoon dried
Large clove garlic
5 cups chicken or beef stock, preferably homemade (see page 13), or canned
15-ounce can pinto beans
8¼-ounce can Italian plum tomatoes
6 tablespoons extra-virgin olive oil, approximately
2 tablespoons vegetable oil
2 tablespoons good-quality red or white wine vinegar, approximately
¾ pound Italian Arborio rice
2 bay leaves
Salt and freshly ground black pepper
¾ cup dry red wine

UTENSILS

Food processor (optional)
Large heavy-gauge nonaluminum saucepan with cover
Small saucepan
Large salad bowl
Heatproof serving bowl
Salad spinner (optional)
Strainer
Measuring cups and spoons
Chef's knife
Paring knife
2 wooden spoons
Wooden spatula
Rubber spatula
Vegetable peeler

START-TO-FINISH STEPS

1. Rinse fresh herbs, if using, and pat dry with paper towels. Chop basil for salad recipe; chop enough marjoram to measure 2 teaspoons for risotto recipe.
2. Follow risotto recipe steps 1 through 9.
3. While rice is cooking, follow salad recipe steps 1 through 3.
4. Follow risotto recipe steps 10 through 12.
5. While risotto is resting, follow salad recipe steps 4 and 5 and serve.
6. Follow risotto recipe steps 13 and 14, and serve.

RECIPES

Escarole, Onion, and Coppa Salad

Medium-size head escarole
Medium-size red onion
2 ounces sliced sweet coppa or capocollo
1 ounce sliced hot coppa or capocollo
6 tablespoons extra-virgin olive oil, approximately
2 tablespoons good-quality red or white wine vinegar, approximately
8 fresh basil leaves, chopped, or ½ teaspoon dried, approximately
Salt
Freshly ground black pepper

1. Remove any tough or bruised outer leaves from escarole. Wash escarole and dry in salad spinner or with paper towels. Tear into bite-sized pieces and place in large salad bowl.

2. Peel and thinly slice onion. Add to escarole, cover bowl with plastic wrap, and refrigerate until ready to serve.

3. Coarsely chop coppa or capocollo; set aside.

4. Just before serving, add olive oil, vinegar, basil, and salt and pepper to taste. Toss salad to combine, taste, and adjust seasoning, adding more oil or vinegar, if desired.

5. Add coppa or capocollo to salad and toss to combine.

Peasant-style Risotto

2 medium-size carrots (about ¾ pound total weight)
2 medium-size yellow onions (about 1 pound total weight)
Small head cabbage (about 1 pound)
1¼ pounds mild home-style Italian sausage
2 tablespoons vegetable oil
8¼-ounce can Italian plum tomatoes
Large clove garlic
2 bay leaves
1 sprig fresh rosemary, or ½ teaspoon dried
2 teaspoons fresh marjoram, chopped, or ½ teaspoon dried
5 cups chicken or beef stock, approximately
15-ounce can pinto beans
¾ cup dry red wine
1½ cups Italian Arborio rice
Salt and freshly ground black pepper

1. Peel carrots and cut into 1-inch-long pieces. Peel and quarter onions. Remove any tough or bruised outer leaves from cabbage. Core, halve, and quarter cabbage.

2. If using food processor, fit with steel blade and process carrots until reduced to small pieces. Remove carrots and coarsely chop cabbage. Remove cabbage, fit processor with slicing disk, and thinly slice onions. Or, use chef's knife to coarsely chop carrots and cabbage, and to slice onions; set aside.

3. Cut sausage into ¼-inch-thick slices; set aside.

4. In large heavy-gauge nonaluminum saucepan, heat oil over medium-high heat. Add carrots, onions, and sausage, and cook, stirring frequently, until onions are golden, about 3 to 5 minutes. Reduce heat, if necessary, to prevent scorching.

5. While onions are cooking, drain 3 plum tomatoes and reserve remaining tomatoes and liquid for another use. Peel and mince garlic.

6. When onions are golden, tilt pan and spoon off all but about 4 tablespoons fat, if necessary. Stir in cabbage, tomatoes, garlic, bay leaves, and herbs, and cook, stirring frequently, over medium-high heat 3 to 4 minutes, or until aromatic.

7. Meanwhile, bring stock to a simmer in small saucepan over high heat. Turn beans into strainer, rinse under cold running water, and drain. Reduce heat under stock and keep hot.

8. Add wine and rice to vegetable-sausage mixture and bring to a boil, stirring to prevent rice from sticking.

9. Reduce heat under rice to medium, stir in 2 cups hot stock, cover pan, and cook, stirring occasionally to prevent sticking, about 10 minutes, or until stock is absorbed and mixture is creamy.

10. Add beans and 2 more cups hot stock to rice and cook, stirring occasionally, another 10 minutes, or until rice is *al dente* and consistency is quite creamy.

11. Remove risotto from heat, cover pan, and set aside to rest for about 15 minutes.

12. Preheat oven to 200 degrees and place heatproof serving bowl in oven to warm.

13. If after resting rice still tastes raw, add another ½ to 1 cup stock, cover, and cook another few minutes until stock is absorbed.

14. Remove bay leaves and rosemary sprig, add salt and pepper to taste, and turn into warm serving bowl.

_____

ADDED TOUCH

These hazelnut meringues, a Piedmontese specialty known as *bruti ma buoni* ("ugly but good"), are an excellent dessert served with espresso.

Hazelnut Meringues

2 cups hazelnuts (about ¾ pound shelled)
¾ cup sugar
½ teaspoon cinnamon
4 egg whites, at room temperature
2 teaspoons unsalted butter
2 tablespoons all-purpose flour, approximately

1. Preheat oven to 350 degrees.

2. Arrange nuts in single layer on large baking sheet and place in oven. Toast nuts, shaking pan occasionally to prevent nuts from scorching, 15 to 20 minutes, or until skins have split open and meat is light golden brown.

3. Remove nuts from oven and set aside. Reduce oven temperature to 250 degrees.

4. Remove skins from nuts by rubbing with clean kitchen towel. Transfer 1 cup nuts to food processor fitted with steel blade and chop coarsely. Turn chopped nuts into medium-size bowl. Process remaining nuts to a paste.

5. Add sugar, cinnamon, and nut paste to chopped nuts, and stir to combine.

6. In large copper or stainless-steel bowl, beat egg whites with electric beater at high speed, or with whisk, until soft peaks form.

7. Add nut mixture to egg whites and fold in until incorporated. Don't worry about the whites deflating.

8. Butter and flour a large cookie sheet; shake off excess flour.

9. Drop about 30 teaspoons batter onto sheet, spacing them about 1 inch apart. Bake 1 hour to 1 hour and 10 minutes, or until firm and dry. When done, turn off oven but do *not* open oven door again.

10. Allow meringues to rest in oven 1 hour, then remove from oven, and cool to room temperature.

Renaissance Almond Broth
Sweet and Savory Broiled Lamb
Herb-Roasted Potatoes

Bowls of almond broth precede the entrée of sliced lamb and roast potatoes garnished with fresh parsley.

Broiled butterflied leg of lamb flavored with a butter that contains crushed juniper berries is an elegant main dish for a special dinner party. The meat of a butterflied leg has been carefully cut off the bone in one large piece so that it resembles a butterfly when laid out. Some sections of the butterflied leg will be thicker than others and will cook more slowly. Use an instant-reading thermometer to test for doneness in the thickest portion. Allow the lamb to rest for 15 minutes while you serve the soup.

Juniper berries, the dried blue fruit of small evergreen shrubs, are available in the spice section of most supermarkets. If you wish to intensify their bittersweet flavor, toast the berries lightly in a dry skillet for a minute or two, then crush them before adding them to the lamb filling.

Balsamic vinegar is a primary flavoring for the roast potatoes. Produced in the Modena province of the Emilia-Romagna region, this unique vinegar has a rich but not cloying flavor with woody and herbal overtones. It is delicious on salads and vegetables. Italian markets and specialty food shops sell this quality vinegar.

WHAT TO DRINK

A dry, fruity red wine suits this menu. The first choice would be a Dolcetto; good alternatives are a French Beaujolais or a California Gamay.

SHOPPING LIST AND STAPLES

2¼- to 2¾-pound loin half of leg of lamb, boned, butterflied, and trimmed
2- to 3-ounce skinless, boneless chicken breast half
2 pounds small red-skinned new potatoes
3 large shallots
2 large cloves garlic plus 1 small clove
Small bunch fresh parsley for garnish (optional)
Small bunch fresh chives or scallions
Small bunch fresh rosemary, or ¼ teaspoon dried
Small bunch fresh sage, or 1 teaspoon dried
Large orange
4 cups homemade chicken stock (see page 13)
4 tablespoons unsalted butter
5 tablespoons extra-virgin olive oil
¼ cup balsamic vinegar
4-ounce can blanched slivered almonds
6 juniper berries
¼ teaspoon ground cloves
Pinch of cinnamon
Salt
Freshly ground black and white pepper
2 tablespoons dry vermouth

UTENSILS

Food processor or blender
Medium-size heavy-gauge nonaluminum saucepan with cover
Small heavy-gauge nonaluminum saucepan
14 x 10-inch roasting pan, preferably heavy-gauge
Broiler pan with rack
Large flat plate
Medium-size bowl
Medium-size fine sieve or strainer
Measuring cups and spoons
Chef's knife
Carving knife
Paring knife
Ladle
2 wooden spoons
Slotted spoon
Instant-reading meat thermometer
Zester

START-TO-FINISH STEPS

Thirty minutes ahead: Place chicken in freezer to chill.

1. Prepare fresh herbs, if using.
2. Follow potatoes recipe steps 1 through 4.
3. Follow lamb recipe steps 1 through 3.
4. Follow soup recipe steps 1 through 3.
5. Follow lamb recipe step 4.
6. Follow potatoes recipe step 5 and lamb recipe step 5; potatoes will roast while lamb broils.
7. Follow soup recipe steps 4 and 5, and lamb recipe step 6.
8. Follow soup recipe step 6.
9. Follow lamb recipe step 7 and potatoes recipe step 6.
10. Follow soup recipe step 7 and serve.
11. Follow lamb recipe step 8 and potatoes recipe step 7 and serve together.

RECIPES

Renaissance Almond Broth

4 cups homemade chicken stock
Small clove garlic
1 cup blanched slivered almonds
Pinch of cinnamon
Small bunch fresh chives or scallions
2- to 3-ounce skinless, boneless chicken breast half, well chilled
Salt and freshly ground white pepper

1. In medium-size heavy-gauge nonaluminum saucepan, bring stock to a boil over medium-high heat.
2. Peel garlic and process with almonds and cinnamon in processor or blender until almonds are powdered.
3. As soon as stock comes to a boil, add almond mixture, cover pan, and remove from heat. Let soup steep, covered, about 30 minutes.
4. Wash and dry chives or scallions. Cut enough chives or scallion greens into 1-inch lengths to measure 2 tablespoons and set aside; reserve remainder for another use.
5. About 10 minutes before serving, remove chicken from freezer. With very sharp carving knife, shave chicken into paper-thin slices, moving knife across the grain and away from you. Arrange slices in single layer on large flat plate and season with salt and pepper to taste.

6. About 5 minutes before serving, strain broth through a fine sieve or strainer set over a medium-size bowl, pressing solids with back of spoon to extract as much liquid as possible. Return soup to saucepan and bring to a simmer over medium heat. Adjust seasoning.

7. Just before serving, add chicken slices to soup (they will cook in soup) and immediately ladle into 4 small bowls. Garnish with chopped chives or scallions and serve.

Sweet and Savory Broiled Lamb

2 large cloves garlic
Large orange
6 juniper berries
4 tablespoons unsalted butter
2 tablespoons dry vermouth
¼ teaspoon chopped fresh rosemary, or ¼ teaspoon dried, plus 4 sprigs for garnish (optional)
¼ teaspoon ground cloves
½ teaspoon freshly ground black pepper
Pinch of salt
3 large shallots
2¼- to 2¾-pound loin half of leg of lamb, boned, butterflied, and trimmed

1. Peel and mince garlic. With zester, grate orange rind, reserving orange for another use. Crush juniper berries by placing them under flat blade of chef's knife and hitting blade sharply with heel of hand.

2. Combine all ingredients except shallots and lamb in small heavy-gauge nonaluminum saucepan and bring to a boil over medium heat. Reduce heat and simmer 2 minutes.

3. While butter-spice blend is simmering, peel and finely chop shallots. Stir shallots into butter, remove pan from heat, and allow to cool.

4. Place lamb on rack in broiler pan. Using sharp paring knife, make about twelve 1- to 1½-inch-wide incisions at an angle, randomly spaced in surface of meat. Using a teaspoon, stuff incisions with butter mixture. Set lamb aside at room temperature.

5. Adjust broiler pan so that lamb is about 6 inches from heating element, and broil 10 minutes.

6. For rare lamb, turn and broil another 5 minutes, or until an instant-reading thermometer inserted into center of thickest part of meat registers 125 degrees; for medium, broil another 2 to 3 minutes or until thermometer registers 140 degrees.

7. Turn off broiler, leave oven door ajar, and let lamb rest about 15 minutes.

8. To serve, thinly slice lamb across grain. Divide slices among dinner plates and garnish each serving with a sprig of rosemary, if desired.

Herb-Roasted Potatoes

2 pounds small red-skinned new potatoes
8 leaves fresh sage, or 1 teaspoon dried
Salt and freshly ground black pepper
5 tablespoons extra-virgin olive oil

¼ cup balsamic vinegar
12 sprigs fresh parsley for garnish (optional)

1. Preheat oven to 425 degrees.

2. Wash potatoes thoroughly under cold running water but do not peel; dry with paper towels.

3. Place potatoes in roasting pan, sprinkle with whole sage leaves and salt and pepper to taste, and drizzle with olive oil. Toss potatoes until evenly coated with oil and seasonings.

4. Place pan on lower oven rack and roast 25 minutes, turning occasionally to prevent sticking.

5. Remove potatoes from oven and turn on broiler. Sprinkle potatoes with 3 tablespoons vinegar and return to oven to continue roasting 15 to 20 minutes.

6. Remove potatoes from oven and cover loosely with foil to keep warm until ready to serve.

7. Use slotted spoon to divide potatoes among dinner plates; sprinkle with remaining vinegar and garnish each serving with pasley sprigs, if desired.

ADDED TOUCH

The success of this baked vegetable dish depends on flavorful, vine-ripened tomatoes, so it is best made in late summer or early autumn.

Baked Zucchini and Tomatoes

3 medium-size zucchini (about 1¼ pounds total weight)
6 plum or other small vine-ripened tomatoes (about 1¼ pounds total weight)
¼ cup extra-virgin olive oil
Salt and freshly ground black pepper
¼ cup loosely packed parsley sprigs
1 tablespoon chopped fresh basil, or 1 teaspoon dried
2 teaspoons fresh marjoram leaves, or ½ teaspoon dried
Small clove garlic, peeled
½ small onion
½-inch-thick slice stale Italian or French bread
1 tablespoon unsalted butter

1. Preheat oven to 400 degrees.

2. Wash zucchini and tomatoes, and dry with paper towels. Trim off ends from zucchini and discard. Cut zucchini on diagonal into ¼-inch-thick slices. Core tomatoes and cut into thin wedges.

3. Coat bottom and sides of medium-size heavy-gauge baking dish with 1 tablespoon olive oil. Arrange alternating slices of zucchini and tomatoes in rows, reversing slant of slices so that adjacent rows slant in opposite directions. Sprinkle with salt and pepper to taste and drizzle with 1 teaspoon olive oil.

4. Combine parsley, basil, marjoram, garlic, onion, bread, and butter in food processor or blender and process until finely minced. Do *not* overprocess. Season mixture to taste with salt and pepper.

5. Spread mixture over vegetables and drizzle with remaining olive oil. Bake about 45 minutes, or until zucchini can be pierced easily with tip of knife.

Prosciutto and Mostarda di Cremona
Minestrone with Chickpeas

For a quick supper, offer prosciutto with mostarda di Cremona *and then bowls of hearty minestrone with crusty bread.*

The elegant appetizer for this easy menu pairs delicate prosciutto with the spicy-sweet fruits of *mostarda di Cremona*. Sold in jars at specialty food shops, these fruits preserved in syrup are flavored with yellow mustard seeds, spices, and sometimes mustard oil. Refrigerate them after opening, and eat them within a month. If *mostarda di Cremona* is unavailable, use whole fresh ripe figs or sweet pears instead.

Both dried Greek oregano and dried *porcini* mushrooms add flavor to the main-course soup. Greek oregano is milder and sweeter than the more commonly sold Mexican variety. Check the label for country of origin. Dried *porcini* mushrooms have a powerful flavor and are sold by the ounce. Select those that are light colored and not too crumbly; they store well for up to two years.

WHAT TO DRINK

To complement this hearty country fare, choose a rustic red wine such as a Sangiovese di Romagna or a red Lacryma Christi.

SHOPPING LIST AND STAPLES

12 thin slices prosciutto (about ¼ pound)
½ pound smoked country-style bacon, sliced
1 pork loin chop (about 6 ounces)
3 medium-size onions (about 1 pound total weight)
Medium-size zucchini
Medium-size carrot
Small bunch celery with leaves
Small head Bibb lettuce
Small bunch fresh parsley
Small bunch fresh basil, or 2 teaspoons dried
2 large cloves garlic
1 lemon or lime (optional), plus additional lemon if using pears
6 ounces Parmesan cheese, preferably imported
6 cups homemade chicken stock (see page 13)
16-ounce can Italian plum tomatoes
16-ounce can tomato purée
15-ounce can chickpeas
3 tablespoons extra-virgin olive oil
12-ounce jar pickled sweet red peppers
13-ounce jar candied mustard fruits, such as mostarda di Cremona, or 4 fresh ripe figs or 4 ripe Bartlett pears
¾ ounce dried porcini mushrooms or cèpes

6 ounces imported pappardelle or other dry, flat, broad pasta
¾ teaspoon dried oregano, preferably Greek
Salt
Freshly ground black pepper

UTENSILS

Food processor (optional)
Large heavy-gauge nonaluminum saucepan or casserole with cover
Large bowl (if using pears)
Small bowl
Salad spinner (optional)
Fine sieve or strainer
Measuring cups and spoons
Chef's knife
Boning knife (optional)
Paring knife
Wooden spoon
Wooden spatula
Grater (if not using processor)
Juicer (if using pears)

START-TO-FINISH STEPS

1. Follow minestrone recipe steps 1 through 6.
2. While vegetables are cooking, follow prosciutto recipe steps 1 through 3.
3. Follow minestrone recipe steps 7 through 12.
4. While pasta is cooking, follow prosciutto recipe steps 4 and 5.
5. Follow minestrone recipe step 13, prosciutto recipe step 6, if using pears, and serve prosciutto and fruits as first course.
6. Follow minestrone recipe step 14 and serve.

RECIPES

Prosciutto and Mostarda di Cremona

Small head Bibb lettuce
12 thin slices prosciutto (about ¼ pound)
1 cup candied mustard fruits, such as mostarda di Cremona, or 4 fresh ripe figs or 4 ripe Bartlett pears
1 lemon or lime (optional), plus additional lemon if using pears

1. Rinse lettuce and dry in salad spinner or with paper towels. Discard any blemished outer leaves. Reserve 4 leaves and refrigerate remainder for another use.

2. Roll each slice of prosciutto into a large cone. Arrange 3 cones on each serving plate, with points together in fan-like shape.

3. If using mustard fruits, select whole fruits in contrasting colors, such as a fig, apricot, or small pear; cut larger fruits into quarters. If using figs, peel carefully (see illustration page 21). If using pears, combine juice of 1 lemon and 1 quart cold water in large bowl. Peel pears, placing each in bowl as you finish peeling to prevent discoloration.

4. Place a lettuce leaf at the point of each prosciutto fan and top leaf with some mustard fruits, or with a whole peeled fig.

5. If mustard fruits are too sweet, halve lemon or lime and squeeze a little juice over each serving. Cover plates loosely with plastic wrap and set in cool place until ready to serve. Do not refrigerate.

6. If using pears, just before serving, drain and divide among plates.

Minestrone with Chickpeas

¾ ounce dried porcini mushrooms or cèpes
Small bunch fresh parsley
1 stalk celery with leaves
Small bunch fresh basil, or 2 teaspoons dried
Medium-size carrot
3 medium-size onions (about 1 pound total weight)
2 large cloves garlic
1 pork loin chop (about 6 ounces)
½ pound smoked country-style bacon, sliced
3 tablespoons extra-virgin olive oil
6 ounces Parmesan cheese, preferably imported
¾ teaspoon dried oregano, preferably Greek
15-ounce can chickpeas
1¼ cups tomato purée
16-ounce can Italian plum tomatoes
Medium-size zucchini
1 cup pickled sweet red peppers
6 cups homemade chicken stock
6 ounces imported pappardelle or other dry, flat, broad
   pasta
Salt and freshly ground black pepper

1. In small bowl, combine dried mushrooms with enough hot water to cover and set aside for at least 15 minutes.

2. Wash parsley, celery, and fresh basil, if using, and dry with paper towels. Reserve ¼ cup firmly packed parsley; refrigerate remainder for another use. Chop enough basil to measure 2 tablespoons. Trim celery and cut into large pieces. Trim and peel carrot; cut into large pieces. Peel onions. Peel and mince garlic.

3. Remove bone from pork chop and discard; coarsely chop meat. Coarsely chop bacon.

4. Heat oil in large heavy-gauge nonaluminum saucepan or casserole over medium-high heat. Add bacon and chopped pork, and sauté, stirring frequently, 5 to 7 minutes or until golden.

5. Meanwhile, if using food processor, grate enough cheese to measure 1½ cups and transfer to small serving bowl. Or, using grater, grate cheese. Clean processor bowl and coarsely chop parsley. Add celery and carrot, and process until medium-fine. With slicing disk, slice onions over vegetables. If using chef's knife, finely chop parsley, celery, and carrot, and thinly slice onions.

6. When meat is done, carefully spoon off all but 3 tablespoons of fat. Add vegetables, stirring to scrape up any brown bits clinging to bottom of pan. Cover, reduce heat to medium-low, and cook 10 minutes.

7. Add mushrooms and, using fine sieve or strainer lined with paper towel, strain soaking liquid into pan. Stir in minced garlic and herbs, and simmer gently 2 to 3 minutes, or until aromatic.

8. Meanwhile, turn chickpeas into sieve or strainer, rinse under cold running water, and drain; set aside.

9. Add tomato purée and plum tomatoes with their liquid to pan, bring to a boil, stirring, and simmer briskly 5 minutes.

10. Wash zucchini and dry. Trim off ends and discard; cut zucchini into ½-inch dice. Drain red peppers and rinse under cold running water. Pat dry with paper towels and cut into ¼-inch-wide strips.

11. Add chickpeas, zucchini, and red pepper strips to pan, and cook, stirring, 1 minute.

12. Stir in chicken stock and bring to a simmer. Add pasta and cook, stirring frequently, 6 to 8 minutes, or until pasta is tender but not mushy.

13. Season with salt and pepper to taste and remove pan from heat. Cover and allow to rest about 10 minutes.

14. If necessary, reheat soup briefly over medium heat before serving. To serve, divide among soup bowls, garnish each with a generous spoonful of Parmesan, and offer remaining cheese separately.

Susan DeRege

Susan DeRege spends long hours in the kitchen almost daily as part of her job, yet she never tires of cooking at home for friends and family. She likes meals that can be prepared ahead, allowing her to spend time with her guests. The three menus she presents here are all based on the cooking of northern Italy.

The pork medallions and the glazed carrots in Menu 1, both Piedmont recipes, can be prepared early in the day, refrigerated, and then quickly reheated for the table. The straw and hay pasta—a recipe from Emilia-Romagna— should be prepared just before dinner.

Menu 3 is a favorite of this cook because it can be made a day ahead and is perfect for either a buffet or a sit-down dinner. The Ligurian artichoke soup is equally good chilled or heated, and the peppers can be served at room temperature or hot. The veal entrée, a Piedmont dish, is named for Count Cavour, the nineteenth-century states-man who came from the region.

Menu 2 is a bit more complicated. The creamy risotto requires constant stirring, so Susan DeRege suggests inviting your guests into the kitchen for a glass of wine while you prepare the meal. The risotto is bound with Parmesan cheese, which also flavors the accompanying Milanese-style chicken. In an Italian home, the endive salad would be served after the main course.

Casual pottery underscores the simplicity of this family meal: pork medallions with a sweet and sour sauce and finger carrots glazed with fruity kirsch. The two-toned pasta dish, tossed with butter, is sprinkled with freshly grated Parmesan and black pepper.

Piedmontese Pork Medallions
Straw and Hay Pasta with Butter Sauce
Carrots with Kirsch

The yellow and green egg noodles may be served as the appetizer or as an accompaniment to the pork medallions and carrots. If the cooked pasta is too dry after adding the Parmesan, tossing the pasta with a little of the hot cooking water will improve the sauce.

The pork medallions simmer gently in milk flavored with rosemary and vinegar. Soft curds may appear when you first add the vinegar to the milk, but after slow cooking they will almost disappear. If you want an especially smooth sauce, blend the milk mixture in your blender or food processor for a few seconds.

WHAT TO DRINK

A dry but not overpowering red wine, such as a Spanna or a Nebbiolo from the Italian Piedmont, would make the best partner for these dishes.

SHOPPING LIST AND STAPLES

1½ pounds boneless pork loin roast from the rib end, cut into 12 medallions and pounded ½ inch thick
Two 12-ounce packages finger carrots, or 14 to 16 regular carrots
Small bunch fresh parsley
Small bunch fresh rosemary, or 1½ teaspoons dried
1½ cups milk
1 stick plus 7 tablespoons unsalted butter
¼ pound Parmesan cheese
1 tablespoon virgin olive oil
3 tablespoons balsamic vinegar
6 ounces green fettuccine plus 6 ounces white
Salt and freshly ground black pepper
¼ cup kirsch

UTENSILS

Food processor (optional)
Stockpot or large kettle
Large heavy-gauge skillet with cover
Medium-size skillet with cover
Large platter
Large ovenproof bowl or casserole
Medium-size ovenproof bowl
Colander
Measuring cups and spoons
Chef's knife

Paring knife
2 wooden spoons
Metal tongs
Vegetable peeler
Grater (if not using processor)

START-TO-FINISH STEPS

1. Follow pork recipe steps 1 through 3 and carrots recipe steps 1 and 2.
2. Follow pasta recipe steps 1 and 2.
3. Follow carrots recipe steps 3 and 4.
4. Follow pasta recipe steps 3 through 7.
5. Follow pork recipe step 4 and serve with pasta and carrots.

RECIPES

Piedmontese Pork Medallions

1 tablespoon virgin olive oil
1 tablespoon unsalted butter
1½ pounds boneless pork loin roast from the rib end, cut into 12 medallions and pounded ½ inch thick
Salt and freshly ground black pepper
1½ cups milk
3 tablespoons balsamic vinegar
3 sprigs fresh rosemary, or 1½ teaspoons dried rosemary, crushed, plus 4 sprigs for garnish (optional)

1. Heat olive oil and butter in large heavy-gauge skillet over high heat. Place about half the medallions in skillet in a single layer and sauté about 3 minutes per side, or until brown. As they brown, transfer medallions to platter and season with salt and pepper to taste. Repeat process for remaining medallions.
2. Lower heat under skillet to medium-high. Add milk slowly to prevent boiling over, stirring and scraping up any browned bits clinging to bottom of pan. Stir in vinegar and rosemary. Cover pan and bring liquid to a boil.
3. When liquid comes to a boil, reduce heat to low. Return all the medallions to skillet, cover partially, and cook, turning occasionally with tongs, 25 to 35 minutes, or until pork is fork-tender and sauce is caramel colored and has reduced to about ½ cup.
4. Remove rosemary sprigs and discard. Divide medallions among plates and top each serving with sauce. Garnish each plate with a sprig of fresh rosemary, if desired.

Straw and Hay Pasta with Butter Sauce

1 stick unsalted butter
1½ tablespoons salt
6 ounces green fettuccine plus 6 ounces white
¼ pound Parmesan cheese
Freshly ground black pepper

1. Bring 4½ quarts cold water to a boil over high heat in stockpot or large kettle. Preheat oven to 200 degrees and place 4 bowls in oven to warm.
2. While water is coming to a boil, cut butter into 8 pieces, transfer to large ovenproof bowl or casserole, and place in oven.
3. Add salt and pasta to boiling water and stir with wooden spoon to blend green and white noodles. Cook pasta 8 to 12 minutes, or just until *al dente*.
4. In food processor or with grater, grate enough Parmesan to measure ¾ cup; set aside.
5. When pasta is almost cooked, remove ¼ cup pasta water and reserve. Turn pasta into colander and drain.
6. Transfer pasta to bowl with melted butter and toss until well coated. Add pepper and ½ cup Parmesan, and toss again. If pasta is still too dry, add a little reserved pasta water and toss to combine.
7. Divide pasta among warm bowls, sprinkle each serving with 1 tablespoon Parmesan, and add a few twists of black pepper; serve remaining cheese separately.

Carrots with Kirsch

Two 12-ounce packages finger carrots, or 14 to 16 regular
    carrots
Small bunch fresh parsley
6 tablespoons butter
½ teaspoon salt
Freshly ground black pepper
¼ cup kirsch

1. Trim and peel carrots. If using finger carrots, leave whole, or halve regular carrots lengthwise, cut crosswise into 2-inch-long pieces, then cut into ½-inch julienne. Wash parsley, dry, and chop enough to measure 2 tablespoons; set aside.
2. In medium-size skillet, bring ½ inch water to a boil over medium-high heat. Add carrots, cover, and cook 6 to 8 minutes, or until they are crisp-tender. Be careful not to let water boil away or carrots will burn.
3. Pour off any water remaining in skillet and lower heat to medium. Add butter, salt, pepper to taste, and kirsch; cook, shaking pan to dissipate alcohol, 3 to 4 minutes, or until carrots are glazed.
4. Turn carrots into medium-size ovenproof bowl, sprinkle with chopped parsley, and keep warm in 200-degree oven until ready to serve.

▬▬▬▬▬
ADDED TOUCH

For this elegant dessert, ripe pears are served in a *zabaglione*, a foamy custard, and drizzled with melted semi-sweet chocolate.

Pears Contessa

4 egg yolks
½ cup sugar
½ cup dry Marsala
Juice of 1 lemon
4 ripe pears with stems intact
½ cup heavy cream
2 ounces imported semi-sweet chocolate

1. Place medium-size bowl and beaters in freezer to chill.
2. Combine egg yolks and sugar in small heavy-gauge nonaluminum saucepan and whisk until thick and fluffy. Gradually add Marsala, whisking until blended.
3. Place saucepan over medium heat and whisk egg mixture briskly until it coats whisk and mounds slightly, about 7 minutes.
4. Turn zabaglione into stainless-steel mixing bowl, cover with plastic wrap, and place in freezer to chill, about 25 minutes.
5. Meanwhile, combine lemon juice and 1 quart cold water in large mixing bowl. Peel pears, placing each in lemon water as you finish peeling it to prevent discoloration.
6. In chilled bowl, beat heavy cream with electric mixer at high speed until stiff. Fold about ¼ cup of chilled zabaglione into the whipped cream, then fold in remaining zabaglione.
7. Pour zabaglione cream into center of gently sloping bowl or 1½-quart soufflé dish. Arrange whole pears around edge, cover with plastic wrap, and refrigerate until ready to serve.
8. Just before serving, melt chocolate in top of double boiler over hot, not boiling, water.
9. Drizzle melted chocolate over pears and zabaglione, and divide among individual plates.

Chicken Breasts Milanese
Risotto with Porcini Mushrooms
Endive Salad with Green Herb Sauce

Crumb-coated chicken breasts, risotto with porcini *mushrooms, and an endive salad are a classic northern Italian meal.*

Instead of using the traditional—and expensive—veal cutlets for this entrée, the cook prepares chicken breasts. However, you can use turkey breasts instead. Dipping the breasts into the seasoned beaten-egg mixture before coating them helps the bread crumbs and Parmesan adhere to the meat.

A good risotto requires patience—here you stir the rice continuously while slowly adding the broth. The trick is not to overcook the dense, creamy mixture because the risotto continues cooking even when removed from the heat.

The endive salad is dressed with a piquant green sauce *(bagnetto verde)*. The sauce is quickly prepared in a food processor or blender and keeps well in the refrigerator for up to a month.

WHAT TO DRINK

This menu deserves either a full-bodied white wine or a light-bodied red. For white, the cook suggests Fiano di Avellino; for red, Grignolino.

SHOPPING LIST AND STAPLES

2 skinless, boneless chicken breasts (about 1½ pounds total weight), halved and trimmed
2 medium-size heads Belgian endive (about ½ pound total weight)
Small bunch watercress
Medium-size carrot
Small yellow onion
Very large clove garlic
Large bunch fresh parsley
Small bunch fresh basil, or ¼ teaspoon dried
Small bunch fresh rosemary, or 2 teaspoons dried, approximately
Small bunch fresh sage, or ½ teaspoon dried
1 lemon
2 eggs
7 tablespoons unsalted butter
¼ pound Parmesan cheese
3¼ cups combined chicken and beef stock, preferably homemade (see page 13), or canned

8-ounce can tomato sauce
2-ounce tin flat anchovies
5 tablespoons corn oil
¼ cup virgin olive oil
1 tablespoon red wine vinegar
3½-ounce jar capers
½-ounce package dried porcini mushrooms
1½ cups Italian Arborio rice
½ cup dry white bread crumbs
1 teaspoon dried thyme
1 teaspoon dried oregano
¼ teaspoon chili powder
Salt and freshly ground black pepper
2 tablespoons dry sherry

UTENSILS

Food processor or blender
Large heavy-gauge skillet
Large heavy-gauge saucepan or enamel-lined casserole
Medium-size saucepan
Medium-size bowl
2 small bowls
Heatproof platter
9-inch pie pan or shallow plate
Small strainer
Measuring cups and spoons
Chef's knife
Paring knife
Wooden spoon
Metal tongs
Vegetable peeler
Grater (if not using processor)

START-TO-FINISH STEPS

1. Prepare parsley, watercress, and fresh herbs, if using. Grate enough Parmesan to measure 1 cup and set aside.
2. Follow risotto recipe steps 1 and 2 and chicken recipe steps 1 through 3.
3. Follow salad recipe steps 1 through 3.
4. Follow herb sauce recipe steps 1 through 3.
5. Follow chicken recipe steps 4 through 6.
6. Follow risotto recipe steps 3 through 7.
7. Follow salad recipe step 4, chicken recipe step 7, and serve with risotto.

RECIPES

Chicken Breasts Milanese

1 lemon
2 eggs
½ cup freshly grated Parmesan cheese
Salt and freshly ground black pepper
2 skinless, boneless chicken breasts (about 1½ pounds total weight), halved and trimmed
½ cup dry white bread crumbs
3 tablespoons unsalted butter

4 tablespoons corn oil
1 sprig fresh rosemary, or ½ teaspoon dried
4 sprigs parsley for garnish (optional)

1. Rinse lemon and dry. Cut into 4 wedges and set aside.
2. In medium-size bowl, combine eggs, ¼ cup of the Parmesan, and salt and pepper to taste, and beat until well blended. Add chicken breasts to egg mixture, turn to coat, and set aside to soak about 10 minutes.
3. Combine remaining cheese and bread crumbs in pie pan; set aside.
4. Preheat oven to 200 degrees. Line heatproof serving platter with paper towels.
5. In large heavy-gauge skillet, heat butter, corn oil, and rosemary over medium-high heat.
6. While fat is heating, dredge each chicken piece in crumb-cheese mixture until evenly coated. When butter stops foaming, add chicken to pan and sauté 4 to 5 minutes per side, or until golden brown. Transfer to paper-towel-lined platter and keep warm in oven until ready to serve.
7. Remove paper towels from platter and garnish chicken with lemon wedges and parsley sprigs, if desired.

Risotto with Porcini Mushrooms

½-ounce package dried porcini mushrooms
Small yellow onion
3¼ cups combined chicken and beef stock
4 tablespoons unsalted butter
1 tablespoon corn oil
Pinch of dried rosemary
1½ cups Italian Arborio rice
2 tablespoons dry sherry
¼ teaspoon salt
½ cup freshly grated Parmesan cheese

1. Rinse mushrooms under cold water. Place them in small bowl, cover with warm water, and soak 20 minutes.
2. Peel and finely chop enough onion to measure 2 tablespoons; set aside.
3. Place serving bowl in 200-degree oven. Bring stock to a boil in medium-size saucepan over high heat, then reduce heat to just maintain a simmer.
4. While stock is heating, combine 3 tablespoons butter, oil, rosemary, and onion in large heavy-gauge saucepan or enamel-lined casserole over medium heat and sauté, stirring occasionally, 5 to 8 minutes, or just until onions are translucent. Add rice and stir until translucent and well coated with fat; do not brown.
5. Lower heat slightly and add hot stock gradually, about ½ cup at a time, stirring constantly after each addition until stock is totally absorbed by rice. Add mushrooms and their soaking liquid to rice. Add sherry and continue stirring over medium-low heat until liquid is absorbed, about 20 minutes.
6. When liquid is absorbed, stir in salt and ¼ cup Parmesan.
7. Remove pan from heat and stir in remaining tablespoon butter. Turn risotto into warm serving bowl and offer remaining cheese separately.

Endive Salad with Green Herb Sauce

2 medium-size heads Belgian endive (about ½ pound total weight)
Medium-size carrot
8 sprigs watercress
Green Herb Sauce (see following recipe)

1. Halve, core, and separate endive leaves. Wash thoroughly and dry with paper towels.

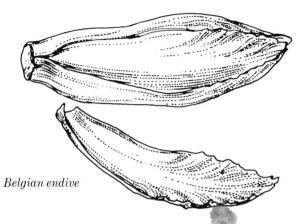

Belgian endive

2. Trim and peel carrot. Halve carrot lengthwise and cut halves into 2-inch-long pieces. Cut each piece into thin matchsticks.
3. Divide endive among individual salad plates and top with watercress. Sprinkle each serving with carrot sticks, cover with plastic wrap, and refrigerate until ready to serve.
4. Just before serving, remove salads from refrigerator and place a generous spoonful of green herb sauce on each plate.

Green Herb Sauce

1 sprig fresh rosemary, or 1½ teaspoons dried
1 tablespoon capers
1 cup fresh parsley, firmly packed
3 leaves fresh sage, or ½ teaspoon dried
2 leaves fresh basil, or ¼ teaspoon dried
1 teaspoon dried thyme
1 teaspoon dried oregano
¼ teaspoon chili powder
1 very large clove garlic
¼ teaspoon salt
¼ teaspoon freshly ground pepper
1 tablespoon red wine vinegar
¼ cup virgin olive oil
2 anchovies
¼ cup tomato sauce

1. Strip leaves from rosemary. Drain capers in small strainer and rinse under cold running water.
2. In food processor or blender, process all ingredients, except olive oil, anchovies, and tomato sauce, until finely chopped.
3. Add remaining ingredients and purée. Adjust seasoning and set aside at room temperature until ready to serve.

50

ADDED TOUCH

For this version of the traditional Italian custard called *panna cotta*, or cooked cream, use a brioche pan to mold the dessert. This classic pan has fluted sides that flare outward from a small round base. Oil the pan before adding the hot custard to make unmolding easier. If you do not have a brioche pan, a 1-quart soufflé dish or glass baking dish works well.

Molded Caramel Custard

¼ cup milk
½ cup plus 3 tablespoons sugar
2 teaspoons unflavored gelatin
4 egg yolks
Pinch of salt
2 tablespoons praline liqueur or Cognac
1½ cups heavy cream

1. Place bowl and beaters for whipping cream in freezer to chill.
2. In small heavy-gauge nonaluminum saucepan, heat milk over medium heat just until it begins to boil. Remove pan from heat.
3. In tea kettle or small saucepan, bring about 1 cup water to a boil.
4. In small heavy-gauge sauté pan, melt ½ cup sugar over low heat, stirring constantly, 8 to 10 minutes, or until melted and straw colored.
5. Remove pan from heat and *very* slowly add 2 tablespoons of the boiling water, stirring constantly, until water is incorporated. Return pan to low heat and cook another 5 minutes, or until caramel thickens.
6. Meanwhile, combine gelatin and 2 tablespoons cold water in small bowl and stir until gelatin dissolves.
7. In medium-size heavy-gauge saucepan, combine egg yolks, remaining sugar, and salt. Add a little hot milk to yolks and stir until blended. Slowly stir in remainder of the milk and cook over low heat, about 5 minutes, or until mixture is thick enough to coat a spoon.
8. Stir in gelatin until incorporated. Stir in two thirds of the warm caramel mixture and the liqueur, cover, and chill in freezer 15 to 20 minutes, or until custard is consistency of stiffly beaten heavy cream.
9. Meanwhile, beat heavy cream until stiff, then gently fold into the chilled custard. Pour into an oiled brioche pan and chill at least 3 hours or overnight.
10. When ready to serve, dip bottom of mold briefly in warm water. Place flat serving plate upside down over pan, tap once sharply against hard surface, and, holding firmly together, invert. Remove pan, drizzle custard with remaining caramel, and serve.

LEFTOVER SUGGESTION

Serve leftover green herb sauce as a dip with crusty Italian bread and raw vegetables, or as a sauce for broiled fish, sausages, or poached meats.

Cream of Artichoke Soup
Veal Scallopini Cavour
Peperonata

The artichoke soup may be served before the entrée of braised veal and strips of sautéed red and yellow peppers.

For this meal the veal is coated evenly with flour, quickly sautéed, and then braised until tender. This technique allows you to use meat from the rump or lower part of the leg rather than expensive top round. The flour browns to a crust and also helps to thicken the braising liquid as the meat cooks. If you assemble all of the ingredients for the veal dish before heating the fat, you can put the meat right into the pan as you dredge the veal. Do not let the meat sit in the flour or the coating will become soggy and stick to the pan rather than to the meat.

For the Italian-style peppers, buy only red and yellow bell peppers that have a uniform, glossy color and thick flesh; they should feel firm and heavy. Refrigerated in a plastic bag, unwashed peppers keep for up to a week.

WHAT TO DRINK

A white Italian Gavi or top-quality Soave, or a red Dolcetto or Chianti Classico, are all good with veal.

SHOPPING LIST AND STAPLES

Eight ¼-inch-thick veal scallops (about 1½ pounds total weight), pounded ⅛ inch thick
2 large red bell peppers (about ¾ pound total weight)
2 large yellow bell peppers (about ¾ pound total weight)
Small yellow onion
Small bunch parsley
1 lemon, plus additional lemon for garnish (optional)

2 eggs
1½ cups milk
½ pint heavy cream
4 tablespoons unsalted butter
Two 9-ounce packages frozen artichoke hearts
⅔ cup virgin olive oil, approximately
½ cup all-purpose flour
1 teaspoon sugar
Salt
Freshly ground black pepper
Freshly ground white pepper
⅓ cup dry white vermouth

UTENSILS

Food processor or blender
Large heavy-gauge skillet with cover
Medium-size skillet with cover
Medium-size nonaluminum saucepan
Ovenproof platter
Ovenproof dish
9-inch pie pan or shallow plate (optional)
2 small bowls
Measuring cups and spoons
Chef's knife
Paring knife
2 wooden spoons
Whisk
Metal tongs

START-TO-FINISH STEPS

One hour ahead: Set out frozen artichoke hearts to thaw for soup recipe.

1. Wash parsley and dry with paper towels. Reserve 4 parsley sprigs for soup garnish, if desired, and chop enough to measure 1 tablespoon for veal recipe; refrigerate remainder for another use. Squeeze enough juice from 1 lemon to measure 3 tablespoons for veal recipe. If using lemon for soup garnish, rinse, dry, and cut remaining lemon crosswise into 8 very thin slices.
2. Follow soup recipe steps 1 through 3.
3. While soup is simmering, follow veal recipe steps 1 through 5 and set pan aside.
4. Follow soup recipe step 4 and peppers recipe steps 1 and 2.
5. Follow soup recipe steps 5 and 6.

6. Follow veal recipe step 6, peppers recipe step 3, and soup recipe step 7.
7. Follow peppers recipe step 4.
8. Follow soup recipe step 8 and serve as first course.
9. Follow veal recipe step 7 and serve with peppers.

RECIPES

Cream of Artichoke Soup

Small yellow onion
Two 9-ounce packages frozen artichoke hearts, thawed
1½ cups milk
1 teaspoon salt
1 teaspoon sugar
2 eggs
1 cup heavy cream
Freshly ground white pepper
8 very thin slices lemon for garnish (optional)
4 parsley sprigs for garnish (optional)

1. Peel and finely chop enough onion to measure ⅓ cup.
2. Combine artichoke hearts, milk, salt, sugar, and chopped onion in medium-size nonaluminum saucepan, and simmer over medium-high heat 20 minutes. Do *not* boil.
3. Meanwhile, separate eggs into 2 small bowls, reserving whites for another use.
4. After 20 minutes, remove pan from heat and allow mixture to cool slightly.
5. Transfer mixture to food processor or blender and purée.
6. Rinse saucepan, return purée to pan, and reheat 3 minutes over medium heat; reduce heat to low, if necessary, to prevent boiling.
7. Add heavy cream to egg yolks and whisk until blended. Slowly add small amount of hot purée to cream mixture, whisking until incorporated. Then add warmed cream mixture to saucepan and stir until blended. Add freshly ground pepper to taste and heat briefly.
8. Divide soup among individual bowls and garnish each serving with 2 lemon slices and parsley sprig, if desired.

Veal Scallopini Cavour

2 tablespoons virgin olive oil
4 tablespoons unsalted butter
½ cup all-purpose flour
Eight ¼-inch-thick veal scallops (about 1½ pounds
    total weight), pounded ⅛ inch thick

Salt and freshly ground black pepper
3 tablespoons lemon juice
⅓ cup dry white vermouth
1 tablespoon chopped parsley

1. Preheat oven to 200 degrees.
2. Combine oil and 3 tablespoons of the butter in large heavy-gauge skillet over medium-high heat.
3. Meanwhile, place flour in pie pan or on plate. Lightly dredge in flour as many scallops as will fit in skillet without crowding; shake off excess flour.
4. When butter stops foaming, add scallops to skillet and sauté about 2 minutes per side, or until browned. Sprinkle with salt and pepper to taste, transfer to platter, and place in oven. Dredge remaining scallops, sauté, and transfer to platter; return to oven.
5. Remove pan from heat and add lemon juice and vermouth, stirring to scrape up any browned bits clinging to bottom of pan.
6. Return scallops and any accumulated juices to pan, cover, and braise over low heat 25 to 30 minutes, or until tender.
7. Transfer scallops to dinner plates. Add chopped parsley and remaining butter to pan and stir until blended. Pour sauce over scallops and serve.

Peperonata

2 large red bell peppers (about ¾ pound total weight)
2 large yellow bell peppers (about ¾ pound total weight)
½ cup virgin olive oil
Salt and freshly ground black pepper

1. Wash peppers and dry. Core, halve, and remove seeds and membranes. Cut peppers lengthwise into ½-inch-thick strips.

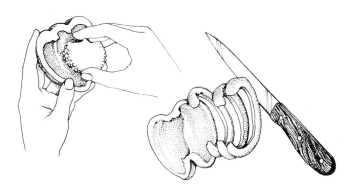

2. Heat olive oil in medium-size skillet over high heat. Add peppers and sauté, stirring, until well coated with oil, 2 to 3 minutes. Cover pan, lower heat to medium, and cook peppers 12 minutes.
3. Remove cover, add salt and pepper to taste, and cook another 10 minutes, or until pan liquid is syrupy.
4. Transfer peppers and syrup to serving dish and keep warm in 200-degree oven until ready to serve.

ADDED TOUCH

For this summertime dessert, use ripe freestone peaches (with easy-to-remove pits) that are firm but yield slightly to pressure. To peel peaches easily, place them in boiling water for 1 minute, then immerse in cold water.

Baked Stuffed Peaches

4 large ripe freestone peaches
½ cup granulated sugar
2 tablespoons cocoa powder
¼ cup blanched almonds, chopped
3 tablespoons grated lemon rind
5 almond macaroons (amaretti), crumbled
1 egg yolk
2 tablespoons Cognac
2 tablespoons unsalted butter

1. Preheat oven to 350 degrees.
2. Peel and halve peaches. Remove pits and discard. Using melon baller or teaspoon, scoop out all but ½ inch of pulp. Place pulp in medium-size mixing bowl.
3. To peach pulp, add ¼ cup sugar, cocoa, almonds, lemon rind, macaroons, egg yolk, and enough Cognac to form a thick paste, and stir to blend.
4. Arrange peach halves in shallow baking dish. Divide filling among halves, dot with butter, and sprinkle with remaining sugar. Bake peaches 20 minutes, or until a slight crust is formed on filling.
5. Divide peaches among individual plates and serve.

LEFTOVER SUGGESTION

Reserve the unused egg whites from the artichoke soup recipe and freeze them until you accumulate enough (about 4 to 6) to make meringues, a popular sweet in Italy (see page 36). For convenience, put each white into a compartment of an ice cube tray and cover the tray tightly with foil.

Nancy Verde Barr

Nancy Barr is particularly interested in recipes from southern Italy, which was her paternal grandparents' home. As a cooking teacher, her ambition is to familiarize Americans with the diversity of southern Italian food. "I want people to know that southerners eat so many more dishes than pizza, lasagna, spaghetti, and meatballs!" she says.

Her Menus 1 and 3 introduce easy but relatively unfamiliar southern Italian dishes. In Menu 1, she serves pasta with a highly seasoned tomato sauce from the region of Calabria and couples it with braised duck and black olives from nearby Basilicata. Menu 3 features a zucchini soup from Naples, lamb chops cooked with mushrooms (a dish popular in Calabria's province of Catanzaro), and broccoli rabe sautéed with olive oil and garlic.

For a change of pace, in Menu 2 Nancy Barr prepares a simple meal from the region of Abruzzo, where pickled vegetables are often cooked with chicken or veal. The tomatoes are stuffed with a mixture of bread crumbs, capers, anchovies, and *soppressata*, a hard Italian salami.

For this informal dinner, present the pieces of browned duck on a large serving platter, then spoon the olives and other sauce ingredients over the top. Penne in a spicy tomato sauce is a traditional southern Italian partner for duck.

54

Braised Duck with Black Olives
Penne with Mushroom Sauce

Most supermarkets sell frozen whole ducks, but because they are increasingly in demand, you can often find them fresh as well. The skin of fresh ducks should be elastic, free of pinfeathers, and should feel well padded with fat. Keep fresh duck loosely wrapped in the coldest part of the refrigerator for up to three days. Frozen ducks should be securely wrapped in sturdy, unbroken plastic wrap. They can be stored frozen for up to three months. Thaw them in the plastic wrap in the refrigerator 24 to 36 hours before cooking; or, if you are in a hurry, put the frozen duck, still wrapped in waterproof plastic, in a pan of cold water and it will be ready for cooking in about three hours.

The penne, or quill-shaped pasta, is served with a simple sauce sparked with hot pepper flakes. Start with a small amount of the flakes, and adjust the seasoning to your taste. If fresh hot chilies are available, try them in place of the pepper flakes. Begin with half a small hot pepper, and increase the amount, if desired. To remove the seeds, wear rubber gloves to protect your hands. The more seeds you leave in, the hotter the flavor.

WHAT TO DRINK

A southern Italian red wine such as the dry and flavorful Taurasi or Aglianico del Vulture complements the strong flavors of the duck.

SHOPPING LIST AND STAPLES

5-pound duckling
¼ pound prosciutto, unsliced
¾ pound mushrooms
2 small onions (about ½ pound total weight)
Small bunch celery
Small bunch carrots
Large clove garlic
1 bunch fresh parsley
Small bunch fresh oregano, or 2 teaspoons dried
¼ pound pecorino Romano or Parmesan cheese
32-ounce can Italian plum tomatoes
6-ounce can pitted black olives
6 tablespoons olive oil
¾ pound penne or similarly shaped pasta
¼ teaspoon red pepper flakes, approximately
1 bay leaf
Salt

Freshly ground black pepper
1 cup dry white wine

UTENSILS

Food processor (optional)
Stockpot
Large sauté pan with cover
Medium-size sauté pan
Broiler rack and pan
Medium-size bowl
Large heatproof serving bowl
Large heatproof serving platter
Colander
Strainer
Measuring cups and spoons
Cleaver
Chef's knife
Paring knife
Wooden spoon
Metal tongs
Grater (if not using processor)
Skewer (optional)
Vegetable peeler (optional)

START-TO-FINISH STEPS

1. Wash parsley and fresh oregano, if using, and dry with paper towels. Chop enough parsley to measure ½ cup for duck recipe and ¼ cup for pasta recipe; chop enough oregano to measure 2 tablespoons for pasta recipe. Peel and chop onions for duck and pasta recipes.
2. Follow duck recipe steps 1 through 6.
3. While duck is broiling, follow pasta recipe steps 1 and 2.
4. Follow duck recipe step 7.
5. While duck is cooking, follow pasta recipe steps 3 through 5.
6. Follow duck recipe steps 8 and 9, and pasta recipe steps 6 through 10.
7. Follow duck recipe step 10 and pasta recipe step 11, and serve together.

RECIPES

Braised Duck with Black Olives

5-pound duckling
Small celery stalk

Small carrot
¼ pound prosciutto, unsliced
1 cup pitted black olives
3 tablespoons olive oil
Small onion, peeled and chopped
1 cup dry white wine
½ cup chopped parsley
1 bay leaf
Salt
Freshly ground black pepper

1. Preheat broiler.
2. Remove any excess fat from cavity of duck. Trim off neck skin. Chop off wing tips and reserve with neck and gizzards for another use. With cleaver, quarter duck: Turn duck skin-side up on cutting surface and cut through the breastbone. Turn duck over, push back breast halves, and cut backbone in two. Next, place each half skin-side up and, feeling for end of rib cage, cut pieces in half just below ribs. Turn quarters skin-side down and, with sharp knife, trim excess skin and any visible fat from each piece.

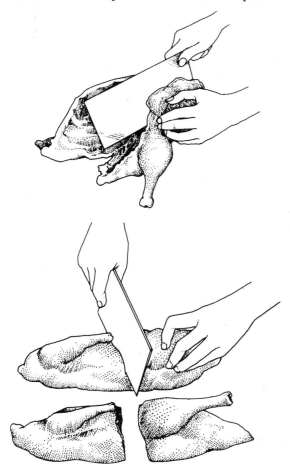

3. Wash celery, dry, and dice enough to measure ¼ cup. Peel and finely dice enough carrot to measure ¼ cup. Chop prosciutto into ¼-inch dice. Slice olives in half; set aside.
4. Place rack in broiler pan. Place duck skin-side up on rack and broil 6 inches away from heating element for 5 minutes.
5. Meanwhile, heat olive oil in large sauté pan over medium heat. Add onion, celery, carrot, and prosciutto and

sauté, stirring occasionally, about 10 minutes, or until onion is golden.
6. After duck has broiled 5 minutes, prick skin all over with skewer or tip of paring knife to release fat, being careful not to penetrate meat. Broil another 5 minutes, pricking skin once more during this time. Turn duck and broil another 5 minutes.
7. Transfer duck to sauté pan with vegetables and prosciutto, add wine, and bring to a boil over high heat. Reduce oven temperature to 200 degrees, leaving door ajar if necessary. Seal pan with sheet of foil, place cover over foil, and cook duck over medium heat 15 minutes.
8. Remove cover and foil, add parsley, bay leaf, olives, and salt and pepper to taste. Reseal pan with foil, re-cover, and cook another 20 minutes, or until tender.
9. Meanwhile, place large heatproof serving platter in oven to warm.
10. When duck is done, transfer to warm platter, top with sauce, and serve.

Penne with Mushroom Sauce

Large clove garlic
¾ pound mushrooms
32-ounce can Italian plum tomatoes
3 tablespoons olive oil
Small onion, peeled and chopped
Salt
¼ cup chopped parsley
2 tablespoons chopped fresh oregano, or
    2 teaspoons dried
¼ teaspoon red pepper flakes, approximately
¼ pound pecorino Romano or Parmesan cheese
¾ pound penne or similarly shaped pasta

1. Peel and coarsely chop garlic. Wipe mushrooms clean with damp paper towels and chop coarsely.
2. In strainer set over medium-size bowl, drain tomatoes; reserve juice. Coarsely chop tomatoes; set aside.
3. Heat oil in medium-size sauté pan over medium heat. Add onion and garlic, and sauté, stirring occasionally, 3 to 4 minutes, or until onions are soft and translucent.
4. Raise heat to high, add mushrooms, and salt to taste; sauté 2 to 3 minutes, or until mushrooms exude liquid.
5. Reduce heat to medium. Add tomatoes, ½ cup reserved tomato juice, parsley, oregano, red pepper flakes, and salt to taste, and simmer 25 minutes, adding more tomato juice if sauce becomes too thick.
6. Bring 2 to 3 quarts salted water to a boil in stockpot over high heat.
7. Meanwhile, in food processor or with grater, grate enough cheese to make 1 cup and set aside.
8. Place large heatproof serving bowl in 200-degree oven to warm.
9. Add penne to boiling water and cook according to package directions until *al dente*.
10. Drain pasta in colander.
11. Turn sauce into warm serving bowl, add drained pasta, and toss to combine. Serve with grated cheese.

Piquant Chicken
Baked Stuffed Tomatoes

For the chicken main dish, the cook suggests butterflying a whole fryer: splitting the bird in half, removing the backbone, and opening the chicken flat. Cooking the chicken this way makes it juicier. Or, have your butcher butterfly the chicken, or substitute a cut-up fryer.

WHAT TO DRINK

A white Lacryma Christi or a top-quality Orvieto would be fine here, or try a California Sauvignon Blanc.

The aromas of the piquant chicken enhance this meal. Spoon some of the sauce with pickled sweet peppers and artichoke hearts over the chicken quarters, and offer a whole baked tomato with each helping.

SHOPPING LIST AND STAPLES

1 frying chicken (about 3 pounds)
¼ pound soppressata or other hard salami
4 medium-size tomatoes (about 1½ pounds total weight)
Small bunch parsley
2 large cloves garlic
9-ounce package frozen artichoke hearts
7 tablespoons olive oil, approximately
12-ounce jar Italian pickled sweet peppers
3½-ounce jar capers
2-ounce tin anchovy fillets
3 slices stale bread, approximately
Salt

Freshly ground black pepper
½ cup dry white wine

UTENSILS

Food processor (optional)
Large heavy-gauge nonaluminum skillet with cover
1½-quart shallow baking dish
Small bowl (if not using processor)
Cake rack
Small strainer
Measuring cups and spoons
Chef's knife
Paring knife
Wooden spoon
Serrated teaspoon (optional)
Metal tongs
Poultry shears (optional)
Grater (if not using processor)

START-TO-FINISH STEPS

One hour ahead: Set out artichoke hearts to thaw for chicken recipe.

1. Follow tomatoes recipe steps 1 and 2.

2. Follow chicken recipe steps 1 through 6.
3. While chicken is cooking, follow tomatoes recipe step 3.
4. Follow chicken recipe step 7 and tomatoes recipe steps 4 through 6.
5. Follow chicken recipe step 8 and tomatoes recipe steps 7 and 8.
6. Follow chicken recipe steps 9 through 12, and serve with tomatoes.

RECIPES

Piquant Chicken

1 frying chicken (about 3 pounds)
2 large cloves garlic
¼ cup olive oil
1 cup Italian pickled sweet peppers, without liquid
½ cup dry white wine
9-ounce package frozen artichoke hearts, thawed
Salt

1. Rinse chicken under cold water and dry with paper towels. To butterfly chicken: Place chicken on cutting surface, breast-side down, with legs pointing toward you. Using poultry shears or chef's knife, cut along each side of backbone as close to the bone as possible. Remove backbone and discard. Turn bird breast-side up and flatten by

striking breastbone with the heel of your hand. Cut off wing tips and tuck wings under.

2. Bruise garlic by placing cloves under flat blade of chef's knife; peel.

3. Heat olive oil in large skillet over medium-low heat. Add garlic and sauté, stirring occasionally, 4 to 6 minutes, or until golden. Discard garlic.

4. Place chicken skin-side down in skillet. Raise heat to medium-high and cook about 8 minutes, or until chicken skin is nicely browned.

5. Meanwhile, cut peppers into ½-inch-wide by 2-inch-long strips; set aside.

6. Turn chicken skin-side up and cook another 7 minutes.

7. Pour off all but 1 tablespoon fat from skillet. Add wine and bring to a boil over high heat; boil 15 seconds. Reduce heat to medium, cover, and cook 15 minutes.

8. Add pepper strips, artichoke hearts, and salt to taste to skillet. Cover and cook another 15 to 20 minutes, or until juices run clear when chicken is pierced with a sharp knife.

9. Toward end of cooking time, place 4 dinner plates under hot running water to warm.

10. When chicken is cooked, remove from pan to cutting surface. With poultry shears or chef's knife, cut chicken into quarters. Dry plates and transfer chicken pieces to them.

11. Raise heat under skillet to high and boil pan juices, stirring to scrape up any browned bits clinging to bottom of pan, until juices are slightly thickened and glossy, 2 to 4 minutes. There should be about ¼ cup of pan juices.

12. Top each serving of chicken with a spoonful of pan juices and some vegetables.

Baked Stuffed Tomatoes

4 medium-size tomatoes (about 1½ pounds total weight)
Salt
3 slices stale bread, approximately
Small bunch parsley
3½-ounce jar capers
2 to 4 anchovy fillets
¼ pound soppressata or other hard salami
3 tablespoons olive oil, approximately
Freshly ground black pepper

1. Preheat oven to 375 degrees.

2. Cut ½-inch-thick slice from tops of tomatoes. Turn each tomato upside down and squeeze gently to remove seeds and juice. Using serrated or regular teaspoon, remove any remaining seeds and enough pulp to make room for stuffing. Sprinkle insides of tomatoes lightly with salt and place upside down on paper-towel-covered cake rack to drain.

3. Trim off crusts from bread and discard. Using food processor or grater, grate enough bread to measure 1 cup crumbs.

4. Rinse parsley and dry with paper towels; finely chop enough to measure ¼ cup. Drain 1 tablespoon capers in small strainer and rinse under cold running water; chop

finely. Drain anchovies; chop finely. Finely chop soppressata to make about 1 cup.

5. Combine parsley, capers, anchovies, soppressata, and bread crumbs in small bowl. Add 1 tablespoon olive oil to mixture and stir until blended. Add pepper to taste but *no* salt; the capers and anchovies provide sufficient saltiness.

6. Divide stuffing among tomato shells.

7. Lightly grease shallow baking dish with some of the remaining oil. Place tomatoes upright in dish and drizzle with 1 or 2 teaspoons olive oil.

8. Bake 20 minutes, or until tomatoes are lightly browned on top.

ADDED TOUCH

Pumate, or dried Italian plum tomatoes, are used in this pasta dish—here in their oil-packed form. Add them sparingly because their concentrated tomato flavor can be overpowering. The richly flavored oil makes a good seasoning for salad dressings or garlic bread.

Linguine with Onions

3 medium-size onions (about ¾ pound total weight)
½ cup plus 3 tablespoons olive oil
2 tablespoons fresh oregano, preferably, or other fresh herb such as marjoram or parsley
9½-ounce jar sun-dried tomatoes in olive oil
¼ pound Kalamata olives
3 slices bread
Salt and freshly ground black pepper
¾ pound linguine, preferably imported

1. Peel and halve onions, then cut crosswise into thin semicircles.

2. Heat ½ cup oil in medium-size sauté pan over medium-low heat. Add onions, cover, and cook until completely softened, about 30 minutes. Do *not* allow onions to brown.

3. Meanwhile, wash fresh oregano and pat dry with paper towels. Coarsely chop enough oregano to measure 2 tablespoons. Cut enough sun-dried tomatoes into ¼-inch-wide strips to measure ½ cup. Pit olives and cut lengthwise into quarters.

4. Trim off crusts from bread and discard. In food processor or with grater, grate enough bread to measure 1 cup crumbs.

5. When onions are ready, stir in oregano, tomatoes, olives, and salt and freshly ground pepper to taste, and cook gently, uncovered, 10 minutes.

6. Meanwhile, in stockpot, bring 3 quarts salted water to a boil over high heat.

7. Heat remaining 3 tablespoons olive oil in small skillet over high heat. Add bread crumbs and toss with fork until golden and toasted, about 4 minutes. Set aside.

8. Transfer onion mixture to large serving bowl.

9. Add linguine to boiling water and cook according to package directions until *al dente*.

10. Drain linguine in colander, turn into bowl with onion mixture, and toss to combine. Sprinkle with toasted bread crumbs and serve.

Zucchini Soup
Lamb Catanzaro-style
Broccoli Rabe

The zucchini soup can precede the main course of broccoli rabe and lamb chops topped with mushrooms and onions.

Whole beaten eggs thicken the zucchini soup. To prevent the eggs from coagulating, first add a small portion of soup to the beaten eggs, stirring continuously. Then blend the warmed eggs into the soup. If the eggs scramble slightly despite this measure, the flavor of the soup will not be affected.

The two-step cooking technique for the broccoli rabe is used throughout Italy. Blanching the vegetable before sautéing it eliminates any bitterness. You may substitute turnip, beet, or mustard greens, but cooking times for these greens vary, so check for doneness.

WHAT TO DRINK

A light red wine would best suit this menu. Choose a young Chianti, Valpolicella, or Bardolino, or a domestic Beaujolais-style Zinfandel.

SHOPPING LIST AND STAPLES

Eight ¾-inch-thick rib lamb chops (about 2¼ pounds total weight)
4 medium-size zucchini (about 1¾ pounds total weight)
1½ pounds broccoli rabe or turnip, beet, or mustard greens
½ pound mushrooms
2 medium-size onions (about ½ pound each)
Small bunch fresh parsley
Small bunch fresh oregano, or 2 teaspoons dried
2 medium-size cloves garlic
2 lemons
2 large eggs
2 ounces pecorino Romano or imported Parmesan cheese
3½ cups beef stock, preferably homemade, or 13¾-ounce can each chicken and beef stock, or 3 cups water
1 cup plus 1 tablespoon olive oil
2 tablespoons lard
2-ounce tin anchovy fillets
3½-ounce jar capers
Four ¾-inch-thick slices Italian bread
¼ cup all-purpose flour, approximately
Salt
Freshly ground black pepper
½ cup dry white wine

UTENSILS

Food processor (optional)
Stockpot
Large heavy-gauge skillet
Medium-size nonaluminum skillet or sauté pan with cover
Large heavy-gauge saucepan
Small saucepan
Large sauté pan with cover
13 x 9-inch baking sheet
Heatproof platter
Medium-size bowl
9-inch pie pan or flat shallow dish
Colander
Small strainer
Measuring cups and spoons
Chef's knife
Paring knife
Wooden spoon
Slotted metal spatula
Ladle
Metal tongs
Grater (if not using processor)

START-TO-FINISH STEPS

1. Follow soup recipe steps 1 through 10.
2. Follow lamb recipe steps 1 through 6.
3. Follow broccoli rabe recipe steps 1 and 2.
4. Follow lamb recipe steps 7 and 8.
5. Follow broccoli rabe recipe steps 3 through 6.
6. Follow lamb recipe step 9 and broccoli rabe recipe step 7.
7. While broccoli rabe cooks, follow soup recipe steps 11 and 12, and serve.
8. Follow lamb recipe steps 10 through 12 and broccoli rabe recipe step 8, and serve.

RECIPES

Zucchini Soup

Small bunch fresh parsley
Small bunch fresh oregano, or 2 teaspoons dried
4 medium-size zucchini (about 1¾ pounds total weight)
Medium-size onion (about ½ pound)
2 ounces pecorino Romano or Parmesan cheese
Four ¾-inch-thick slices Italian bread
2 tablespoons lard
2 tablespoons olive oil
3½ cups beef stock, or 13¾-ounce can each chicken and beef stock, or 3 cups water
Salt
Freshly ground black pepper
2 large eggs

1. Preheat oven to 350 degrees.
2. Wash parsley and fresh oregano and dry with paper towels. Chop enough parsley to measure ¼ cup. Chop enough oregano to measure 2 tablespoons. Wash zucchini, dry, and trim off ends. Cut zucchini into ½-inch slices. Peel and slice onion crosswise into thin rounds.
3. In food processor or with grater, grate enough cheese to measure ⅓ cup; set aside.
4. Arrange bread in single layer on baking sheet and toast in oven 5 minutes.
5. While bread is toasting, combine lard and olive oil in large heavy-gauge saucepan over medium heat. Add onion and sauté, stirring occasionally, 4 to 5 minutes, or until soft and translucent.

6. Turn bread and toast on other side another 5 minutes.

7. Meanwhile, bring stock to a gentle simmer in small saucepan over medium heat.

8. Add zucchini to onion and toss to combine. Add hot stock and salt and pepper to taste, and simmer gently 15 to 20 minutes, or until zucchini are tender.

9. Meanwhile, remove bread from oven and set aside. Reduce oven temperature to 200 degrees.

10. In medium-size bowl, combine eggs, grated cheese, and chopped herbs, and beat until blended; set aside.

11. Beating continuously with wooden spoon, slowly add 1 cup of hot soup to egg mixture; then gradually add egg mixture to soup, stirring continuously until blended. Heat soup just to a simmer; do *not* boil.

12. Place a slice of toasted bread in each of 4 soup bowls. Divide soup among bowls, and serve.

Lamb Catanzaro-style

Medium-size onion (about ½ pound)
½ pound mushrooms
3½-ounce jar capers
2-ounce tin anchovy fillets
½ cup plus 3 tablespoons olive oil
¼ cup all-purpose flour, approximately
Eight ¾-inch-thick rib lamb chops (about 2¼
    pounds total weight)
Salt
Freshly ground black pepper
½ cup dry white wine

1. Peel and finely chop enough onion to measure ¼ cup. Wipe mushrooms clean with damp paper towels and cut into ⅛-inch-thick slices.

2. Rinse 2 tablespoons capers in small strainer under cold running water and drain. Rinse 3 anchovy fillets under cold running water and dry with paper towels. Coarsely chop capers and anchovies.

3. Heat 3 tablespoons olive oil in medium-size non-aluminum skillet over medium heat. Add onion and sauté, stirring occasionally, 5 to 8 minutes, or until onion is golden.

4. Meanwhile, place flour in pie pan or flat shallow dish. Trim off excess fat from lamb chops and dust chops lightly with flour.

5. Heat remaining ½ cup olive oil in large heavy-gauge skillet over medium-high heat. Add chops and brown 5 to 6 minutes on one side.

6. While chops are cooking, add mushrooms, and salt and pepper to taste to onions, and sauté, stirring occasionally, 3 to 5 minutes, or until mushrooms release their juices.

7. Using metal tongs, turn chops and brown on other side another 5 to 6 minutes.

8. Cover onion-mushroom mixture, remove pan from heat, and set aside.

9. With slotted metal spatula, transfer chops to heatproof platter, sprinkle with salt and pepper, and place in 200 degree oven.

10. Pour off all but 2 tablespoons of fat from skillet. Return skillet to high heat, add wine and any juices that have accumulated around lamb chops, and bring to a boil, scraping up any browned bits clinging to bottom of pan. Continue boiling 2 to 3 minutes, or until liquid is reduced by half.

11. Add reduced pan juices to onion-mushroom mixture and stir to combine. Reheat briefly over medium heat.

12. Divide lamb chops among 4 dinner plates and top each serving with some of the onion-mushroom mixture.

Broccoli Rabe

Salt
1½ pounds broccoli rabe or turnip, beet, or
    mustard greens
2 medium-size cloves garlic
2 lemons
¼ cup olive oil
Freshly ground black pepper

1. Bring 2 quarts of lightly salted water to a boil in stockpot over high heat.

2. Meanwhile, remove tough outer leaves from broccoli rabe and discard. With paring knife, peel stems and wash broccoli rabe thoroughly under cold running water. Cut each stalk into thirds.

Broccoli rabe

3. Add broccoli rabe to boiling water and cook 3 minutes.

4. While broccoli rabe is cooking, bruise garlic under flat blade of chef's knife and peel. Rinse 1 lemon, dry, and cut into 8 wedges; set aside. Halve remaining lemon. Squeeze juice of one half, and set aside; reserve other half for another use.

5. Turn broccoli rabe into colander, refresh under cold running water, and drain. Wrap in clean kitchen towel or paper towels to dry.

6. Heat olive oil in large sauté pan over medium heat. Add garlic and sauté 2 to 3 minutes, or until lightly golden.

7. Add broccoli rabe, and salt and pepper to taste, cover pan, and cook 10 to 12 minutes, or until broccoli rabe is fork-tender.

8. Remove garlic and discard. Sprinkle broccoli rabe with lemon juice, divide among 4 dinner plates, and serve with lemon wedges.

Robert Pucci

MENU 1 (Right)
Braised Beef Tenderloin in Wine Sauce
Potatoes Parmigiana
Sautéed Vegetables

MENU 2
Linguine with Clam Sauce
Fillets of Flounder Sorrento
Sautéed Spinach with Pine Nuts and Raisins

MENU 3
Angel Hair Pasta with Onions and Pepper Strips
Veal Scallopini Marsala
Warm Vegetable Salad

P roperly prepared Italian food is particularly wholesome and often low in fat, qualities that Robert Pucci's three menus highlight. For Menu 1, an adaptation of a restaurant meal he had in Rome, he serves an entrée of braised tenderloin steaks, mashed potatoes flavored with grated Parmesan cheese, and a mix of fresh vegetables. Although in Italy carbohydrates are rarely eaten with the main course, mashed potatoes with braised meat are an exception.

Menu 2, an amalgam of many striking Italian flavors, begins with a Venetian-style linguine that combines freshly grated Parmesan cheese with baby clams. Flounder fillets in a zesty tomato sauce with capers and black olives (the recipe is named for Sorrento, a town near Naples) and Ligurian spinach, pine nuts, and raisins are presented after the pasta.

Well-balanced in taste, texture, and color, Menu 3 can be planned with the angel hair pasta as the first course, followed by veal Marsala and a salad of steamed vegetables marinated in a garlic and basil vinaigrette. Or serve the salad as the appetizer and the pasta and veal together.

For an elegant dinner for company, serve individual tenderloin steaks with a creamy wine sauce, sautéed vegetables, and mashed potatoes with Parmesan and parsley.

Braised Beef Tenderloin in Wine Sauce
Potatoes Parmigiana
Sautéed Vegetables

Beef tenderloin steaks are served here with a cream-enriched Marsala and red wine sauce. Dry Marsalas are preferable for red meat dishes.

For the fluffiest mashed potatoes, use a high-starch potato variety such as russet. Long ovals with rough surfaces, russets—like all potatoes—should be clean, firm, and smooth without wilt, soft dark spots, a green tinge, or sprouts. Never store potatoes in the refrigerator because cold temperatures convert the starch into sugar, making the potatoes too sweet.

WHAT TO DRINK

The cook suggests a full-bodied Chianti Classico to complement this menu; a Spanna or Nebbiolo is also fine.

SHOPPING LIST AND STAPLES

Four 1-inch-thick beef tenderloin steaks (about 1¼ to 1½ pounds total weight)
2 pounds boiling potatoes
½ pound carrots
¼ pound summer squash, if available
¼ pound very small zucchini, or ½ pound, if not using summer squash
½ pound asparagus, if available, or snow peas
Small onion
1 yellow bell pepper
1 red bell pepper
Small bunch parsley
3 large cloves garlic
1 lemon
6-ounce can tomato paste
½ pint heavy cream
5 tablespoons unsalted butter
2 ounces Parmesan cheese, preferably imported
5 tablespoons virgin olive oil
1 tablespoon fennel seeds
½ teaspoon red pepper flakes
¼ teaspoon freshly grated nutmeg
Salt and freshly ground black pepper
½ cup dry Marsala, preferably Florio or Rallo
½ cup full-bodied dry red wine, such as Chianti

UTENSILS

Large heavy-gauge skillet
Medium-size heavy gauge skillet
Large saucepan
Medium-size saucepan
2-quart heatproof casserole
Platter
2 large bowls, 1 heatproof
2 small bowls
Vegetable steamer
Colander
Strainer
Measuring cups and spoons
Chef's knife
Paring knife
Wooden spoon
Metal spatula
Rubber spatula
Whisk
Metal tongs
Vegetable peeler
Grater
Electric mixer
Rolling pin

START-TO-FINISH STEPS

Thirty minutes ahead: Set out ½ cup heavy cream to bring to room temperature for potatoes recipe.

1. Peel and mince garlic for beef and vegetables recipes; peel garlic clove for potatoes recipe.
2. Follow potatoes recipe steps 1 through 5.
3. Follow vegetables recipe steps 1 and 2.
4. Follow potatoes recipe steps 6 through 9.
5. Follow vegetables recipe steps 3 through 7.
6. Follow beef recipe steps 1 through 9.
7. Follow vegetables recipe steps 8 through 10.
8. Follow beef recipe steps 10 through 12, potatoes recipe step 10, and serve with vegetables.

RECIPES

Braised Beef Tenderloin in Wine Sauce

1 tablespoon fennel seeds
2 tablespoons unsalted butter
2 tablespoons virgin olive oil
Four 1-inch-thick beef tenderloin steaks (about 1¼ to 1½ pounds total weight)

Salt
2 teaspoons finely minced garlic
½ teaspoon red pepper flakes
1 tablespoon tomato paste
½ cup dry Marsala, preferably Florio or Rallo
½ cup full-bodied dry red wine, such as Chianti
½ cup heavy cream, approximately

1. Preheat oven to 200 degrees.
2. Crush fennel seeds between 2 sheets of waxed paper with rolling pin.
3. Combine butter and oil in medium-size heavy-gauge skillet over high heat. Add steaks and cook 2 to 3 minutes per side, or until brown.
4. Using tongs, transfer steaks to platter and salt lightly. Cover loosely with foil to keep warm and set aside.
5. Reduce heat under skillet to medium-low. Stir in garlic, red pepper flakes, and crushed fennel, and cook 1 minute.
6. Add tomato paste; cook, stirring, another 2 minutes.
7. Increase heat to medium, add Marsala and red wine, and cook about 5 minutes, or until reduced by half.
8. Place 4 dinner plates in oven to warm.
9. Reduce heat under skillet to low, stir in heavy cream to taste, and cook about 5 minutes, or until sauce is thick enough to coat back of spoon.
10. Strain sauce into small bowl and return to skillet.
11. Stir in any juices that have accumulated on platter with steaks and return steaks to skillet. Over low heat, reheat steaks about 2 minutes, turning once to coat with sauce. If sauce separates, whisk in a bit more cream.
12. Place 1 steak on each dinner plate and top with sauce.

Potatoes Parmigiana

Large clove garlic, peeled
Salt
2 pounds boiling potatoes
Small bunch parsley
2 ounces Parmesan cheese, preferably imported
½ cup heavy cream, at room temperature
¼ teaspoon freshly grated nutmeg
Freshly ground black pepper

1. Crush garlic under flat blade of chef's knife.
2. Bring 2 quarts water, ½ teaspoon salt, and crushed garlic to a boil in large saucepan over medium-high heat.
3. Fill large bowl half full with cold water. Peel potatoes, placing in bowl of water; cut into 1-inch chunks.
4. Add potatoes to boiling water and cook 15 to 20 minutes, or until tender when pierced with a sharp knife.
5. Meanwhile, rinse parsley, dry with paper towels, and chop enough to measure 2 tablespoons. Using grater, grate cheese to measure ½ cup. Place 1 tablespoon parsley and all of the grated cheese in small bowl and toss with fork; set aside. Reserve remaining chopped parsley.
6. Drain potatoes, reserving ½ cup cooking water. Transfer potatoes to large heatproof bowl.
7. With electric mixer, beat potatoes until smooth, adding a bit of reserved cooking water if they seem dry.

8. Add cream, nutmeg, and salt and pepper to taste, and beat until blended.
9. Add Parmesan and parsley and beat to combine. Adjust seasoning, cover potatoes loosely with foil, and keep warm in 200-degree oven until ready to serve.
10. Divide mashed potatoes among dinner plates, sprinkle with reserved parsley, and serve.

Sautéed Vegetables

½ pound carrots
½ pound asparagus, if available, or snow peas
¼ pound summer squash, if available
¼ pound very small zucchini, or ½ pound, if not using summer squash
1 yellow bell pepper
1 red bell pepper
Small onion
3 tablespoons unsalted butter
3 tablespoons olive oil
Large clove garlic, finely minced
1 lemon
Salt and freshly ground black pepper

1. Wash vegetables and dry with paper towels. Peel carrots and cut into 1½-inch-long pieces. Halve pieces lengthwise and cut into ¼-inch-thick julienne. Break off tough bottom ends of asparagus and peel, if desired. Trim off ends of summer squash and zucchini, and discard. Cut crosswise into 1½-inch-long pieces. Halve pieces lengthwise. Remove seeds with teaspoon and discard. Cut summer squash and zucchini into ¼-inch-thick julienne. Halve, core, and seed bell peppers. Cut into ¼-inch-thick strips. Peel and quarter onion; cut lengthwise into ⅛-inch-thick slivers.
2. In medium-size saucepan fitted with vegetable steamer, bring to a boil enough water to come just up to but not above bottom of steamer.
3. Add carrots and steam 1½ to 2 minutes, or until crisp-tender. Transfer carrots to colander, refresh under cold running water, and drain.
4. Add asparagus to pan and steam 2 to 3 minutes.
5. Transfer cooked carrots to plate and set aside.
6. Transfer asparagus to colander, refresh under cold running water, and drain.
7. Add summer squash and zucchini to pan and steam 1 minute. Transfer to colander, refresh under cold running water, and drain.
8. Combine butter and oil in large heavy-gauge skillet over medium heat. Add onion and sauté, stirring, 2 minutes. Then add garlic and sauté 1 minute.
9. One at a time, add vegetables, stirring after each addition to combine, and cook 2 to 3 minutes, or just until vegetables are heated through.
10. Meanwhile, squeeze enough lemon juice to measure 1 tablespoon. Add lemon juice and salt and pepper to taste to vegetables. Turn vegetables into heatproof casserole, cover loosely with foil, and keep warm in 200-degree oven until ready to serve.

Linguine with Clam Sauce
Fillets of Flounder Sorrento
Sautéed Spinach with Pine Nuts and Raisins

Baked flounder fillets in a sauce of onions, black olives, and tomatoes are accompanied by sautéed spinach with pine nuts and raisins. Mixing white and green linguine gives the pasta dish greater visual appeal.

F lounder has tender, white flesh and a delicate flavor. Select firm moist fillets with a fresh aroma, and refrigerate them well-wrapped until ready to use. To prevent sticking, coat the baking dish with sauce before adding the fish. Baking the fillets briefly keeps them from toughening. Cod, sole, or halibut is also good in this recipe.

WHAT TO DRINK

A crisp, dry white wine such as Verdicchio is the best choice here. Greco di Tufo and white Lacryma Christi are suitable options, as is a good French Chablis.

SHOPPING LIST AND STAPLES

4 fillets of flounder (1¼ to 1½ pounds total weight)
1½ pounds spinach
Large onion
Small bunch fresh parsley
Small bunch fresh oregano, or 1 teaspoon dried
2 large cloves garlic
8¼-ounce can Italian plum tomatoes
10-ounce can whole baby clams
1 stick unsalted butter, approximately
¼ pound Parmesan cheese, preferably imported
5 tablespoons olive oil
10-ounce jar oil-cured black olives
2-ounce tin rolled anchovies
3½-ounce jar capers
2-ounce jar pine nuts
¾ pound white and green linguine combined
15-ounce box golden raisins
¼ teaspoon freshly grated nutmeg
Salt and freshly ground black pepper,
⅔ cup dry white wine, approximately

UTENSILS

Food processor (optional)
Stockpot
Large skillet
Medium-size skillet with cover
Medium-size sauté pan
13 x 9-inch baking dish
Small saucepan
Colander
Strainer

Measuring cups and spoons
Chef's knife
Paring knife
2 wooden spoons
Wide metal spatula
Grater (if not using processor)

START-TO-FINISH STEPS

1. Peel and mince garlic for linguine, fish, and spinach recipes. Grate Parmesan for linguine and spinach recipes.
2. Follow fish recipe steps 1 and 2, and spinach recipe steps 1 and 2.
3. Follow fish recipe steps 3 through 5.
4. Follow spinach recipe step 3 and linguine recipe steps 1 through 5.
5. While sauce is simmering, follow fish recipe step 6.
6. Follow linguine recipe steps 6 and 7, and fish recipe step 7.
7. Follow linguine recipe step 8 and serve as first course.
8. Follow fish recipe steps 8 through 10.
9. While fish is baking, follow spinach recipe steps 4 through 6.
10. Follow fish recipe steps 11 and 12.
11. Follow spinach recipe steps 7 through 9, fish recipe step 13, and serve.

RECIPES

Linguine with Clam Sauce

Small bunch fresh parsley
2 tablespoons capers
Salt
2 tablespoons olive oil
4 tablespoons unsalted butter, approximately
1½ teaspoons minced garlic
10-ounce can whole baby clams
⅓ cup dry white wine
¾ pound white and green linguine combined
½ cup freshly grated Parmesan cheese
Freshly ground black pepper

1. Wash parsley and dry with paper towels. Chop enough to measure 4 tablespoons; reserve remainder for another use. Drain capers and chop, if large; set aside.
2. Bring 2 quarts salted water to a boil in stockpot over medium-high heat.
3. Meanwhile, combine oil and 2 tablespoons butter in large skillet over low heat. Add garlic and sauté 2 minutes.
4. Add 2 tablespoons parsley to skillet; sauté 30 seconds.
5. Strain canned clam broth into skillet; reserve clams. Stir in white wine and simmer, uncovered, 10 to 15 minutes, or until thick.
6. Add linguine to boiling water and cook 8 to 10 minutes, or according to package directions for desired doneness.
7. Add capers and clams to sauce, and simmer about 2 minutes, or just until heated through.
8. Turn pasta into colander and drain. Add pasta to sauce

in skillet and toss to combine. Add Parmesan, remaining parsley, 1 or 2 tablespoons of remaining butter, and pepper to taste, and toss. Turn into large bowl and serve.

Fillets of Flounder Sorrento

Small bunch fresh oregano, or 1 teaspoon dried
Large onion
8¼-ounce can Italian plum tomatoes
2 tablespoons capers
3 tablespoons olive oil
2 teaspoons minced garlic
Salt and freshly ground black pepper
¼ cup oil-cured black olives
4 fillets of flounder (1¼ to 1½ pounds total weight)
½ cup dry white wine

1. If using fresh oregano, wash and dry with paper towels. Chop enough to measure 1 tablespoon, reserving remainder for another use. Peel and thinly slice onion. Drain tomatoes, reserving juice for another use, and chop enough to measure 1 cup. Drain capers.
2. Heat olive oil in medium-size skillet over medium heat. Add onion and sauté, stirring occasionally, about 8 minutes, or until golden.
3. Add garlic and sauté 1 minute.
4. Add tomatoes, oregano, and salt and pepper to taste, reduce heat to medium-low, and simmer about 15 minutes, or until sauce is thickened.
5. Meanwhile, preheat oven to 450 degrees.
6. Pit olives and chop coarsely. Add olives and capers to sauce and simmer another 5 minutes.
7. Remove pan from heat, cover, and set aside.
8. Wash fillets and dry with paper towels.
9. Coat baking dish with spoonful of sauce. One at a time, arrange fillets in dish: Top each with a spoonful of sauce and then overlap with another fillet. Pour wine over fish and bake 6 to 8 minutes, or until fish flakes easily when tested with fork.
10. Place serving platter under hot water to warm.
11. When fish is done, dry platter. With wide metal spatula, gently transfer fillets with sauce to warm platter.
12. Strain pan juices into small saucepan; reduce over high heat 2 to 3 minutes, or until slightly thickened.
13. Pour reduced pan juices over fillets and serve.

Sautéed Spinach with Pine Nuts and Raisins

1½ pounds spinach
4 tablespoons unsalted butter
1 teaspoon minced garlic
2 rolled anchovies
2 tablespoons pine nuts
¼ teaspoon freshly grated nutmeg
Salt and freshly ground black pepper
2 tablespoons golden raisins
2 tablespoons freshly grated Parmesan cheese

1. Remove stems from spinach and discard. Wash spinach thoroughly in several changes of cold water; do *not* dry.
2. Add spinach to stockpot and cook over medium-low

heat about 5 minutes, or until wilted.

3. Turn spinach into colander, cool under cold running water, and press out excess water with back of spoon. Chop spinach coarsely; set aside.

4. Heat butter in medium-size sauté pan over low heat. Add garlic and sauté about 1 minute.

5. Add anchovies and mash into butter with back of spoon.

6. Add spinach and sauté over low heat, stirring occasionally, 5 minutes, or until moisture has evaporated. Place serving bowl under hot running water to warm.

7. Add pine nuts and nutmeg to spinach, and salt and pepper to taste; stir to combine.

8. Add raisins to mixture and continue cooking just until raisins are heated through, about 1 minute.

9. Dry serving bowl. Add Parmesan to spinach, stir to combine, and turn into warm bowl.

ADDED TOUCH

This elaborate confection of liqueur-soaked cake with custard filling should sit in the refrigerator for 3 to 7 days.

Zuppa Inglese

Cake:
6 extra-large eggs, at room temperature
1¼ cups granulated sugar
2 cups all-purpose flour
6 tablespoons unsalted butter, clarified (see page 12)
1 teaspoon vanilla extract

Pastry creams:
2½ cups milk
4 large egg yolks
¼ cup granulated sugar
¼ cup all-purpose flour
Grated peel of 1 lemon and 1 orange
⅓ cup grated bitter chocolate (1 ounce)
½ teaspoon vanilla extract (optional)
3 tablespoons candied citrus peel, or 1 tablespoon each dark raisins, golden raisins, and currants
½ cup dark rum

¼ cup flavored liqueur, such as Cointreau, Amaretto, or kirsch or brandy

Frosting:
1¼ cups heavy cream
2 tablespoons granulated sugar
2 tablespoons rum, brandy or flavored liqueur

1. Preheat oven to 350 degrees.

2. Place whole eggs in large mixing bowl with enough hot water to cover; set bowl in baking pan partially filled with hot water. Set aside for at least 15 minutes.

3. Trace 2 outlines of 9-inch round cake pan on sheet of waxed paper. With scissors, cut out rounds.

4. Butter two 9-inch round cake pans. Line each pan with waxed paper; butter paper. Place about 1 tablespoon flour in each pan; tilt and rotate pans until well coated; shake off excess flour.

5. Drain eggs and pour off water in bowl; dry bowl. Crack eggs into bowl and beat with electric mixer at high speed about 5 minutes, or until eggs begin to thicken.

6. Still beating, gradually add 1¼ cups sugar and beat another 5 minutes, or until mixture is smooth and thickened.

7. Sift one third of the 2 cups flour over egg mixture and gently fold in, being careful to incorporate the flour without deflating the eggs. In same manner, sift and fold in remaining flour in two batches.

8. In same manner, fold in clarified butter and 1 teaspoon vanilla making sure they are totally incorporated and batter is uniform in texture.

9. Divide batter between pans and bake 25 to 30 minutes, or until toothpick inserted in center comes out clean.

10. Meanwhile, to make pastry creams, heat milk in small saucepan over medium heat.

11. Whisk egg yolks in medium-size saucepan until blended. Whisk in ¼ cup sugar and ¼ cup flour. Still whisking, add warm milk in a slow, steady stream; cook, stirring, over low heat about 10 minutes, or until thick.

12. Off heat, return half of mixture to saucepan used to heat milk, stir in lemon and orange peel. Set aside.

13. Add grated chocolate to remaining half of mixture and whisk off heat until chocolate is melted and totally incorporated. Whisk in ½ teaspoon vanilla extract, if desired. Set aside to cool.

14. Combine candied citrus peel and ¼ cup rum; set aside.

15. Transfer cake to rack and let cool 10 minutes.

16. Turn cake layers out onto rack. Remove waxed paper and let cool completely, about 15 minutes.

17. When cake is cool, cut each layer in half horizontally. You will need 3 half-layers for the dessert.

18. To assemble the dessert, line bottom and sides of straight-sided bowl or springform pan with cheesecloth moistened in water. Place one half-layer, cut-side up, in bottom of bowl or pan. Using pastry brush, brush cake with remaining ¼ cup rum. Top with chocolate pastry cream and smooth out with metal cake spatula.

19. Place another half-layer, cut-side up, over pastry cream, brush with half of the liqueur or brandy.

20. Drain off rum from candied peel and add peel to lemon-orange pastry cream. Turn lemon-orange cream out onto cake and smooth out.

21. Top with remaining half-layer of cake, cut-side down, and brush with remaining liqueur or brandy. Cover bowl or pan with sheet of foil, place in refrigerator, and cover with plate that fits inside of bowl or pan. Place 5-pound weight, such as bag of flour or sugar, on top of plate. Let cake rest in refrigerator 3 to 7 days before serving.

22. To unmold dessert, place flat serving dish over bowl or pan; holding firmly together, invert. Gently pull downward on cheesecloth; then lift off bowl or remove sides of springform pan. Remove cheesecloth.

23. For frosting, beat heavy cream with electric mixer at high speed until soft peaks form. Still beating, add sugar, rum, or liqueur; continue to beat until stiff.

24. Frost dessert with whipped cream and serve.

Angel Hair Pasta with Onions and Pepper Strips
Veal Scallopini Marsala
Warm Vegetable Salad

Veal scallops subtly flavored with Marsala and a warm vegetable salad complement a bowl of angel hair pasta.

Veal scallopini, or scallops, are thin slices cut from the leg, which are pounded to flatten them for quick and uniform cooking. Remove any fat or filament before sprinkling the veal with flour. Scallops are best fried or sautéed briefly over medium heat so that they cook through quickly. You can also use scallops of turkey.

WHAT TO DRINK

Try a firm, somewhat fruity white wine, such as an Italian Chardonnay or a Tocai from Friuli.

SHOPPING LIST AND STAPLES

8 veal scallops (about 1¼ pounds total weight), pounded ¼ inch thick
1 pint cherry tomatoes
½ pound zucchini
½ pound summer squash
½ pound carrots
1 red bell pepper
1 pound white or yellow onions
Small red onion
Small bunch fresh parsley
Small bunch fresh basil, or 2 to 3 teaspoons dried
Large clove garlic
1 lemon
1 stick unsalted butter, approximately
2 ounces Parmesan cheese, preferably imported
¾ cup olive oil, preferably imported
2 tablespoons vegetable oil or light olive oil
2 tablespoons red wine vinegar, preferably imported
½ pound angel hair pasta (capelli d'angelo) or capellini
¼ cup all-purpose flour, approximately
Pinch of sugar
Salt and freshly ground black pepper
½ cup sweet Marsala

UTENSILS

Stockpot
Large heavy-gauge skillet
Large flameproof casserole with cover
Medium-size saucepan
Small saucepan
Heatproof platter
Large heatproof bowl
9-inch pie pan or shallow dish
Colander
Vegetable steamer
Measuring cups and spoons
Chef's knife
Paring knife
2 wooden spoons
Garlic press
Metal tongs
Vegetable peeler
Grater

START-TO-FINISH STEPS

1. Wash parsley and fresh basil, if using, and dry with paper towels. Chop enough parsley to measure 2 tablespoons for veal recipe and 2 tablespoons for pasta recipe. Chop enough basil to measure 3 tablespoons for salad recipe and refrigerate remainder for another use.
2. Follow pasta recipe steps 1 through 4.
3. Follow salad recipe steps 1 through 4.
4. Follow veal recipe steps 1 through 4.
5. Follow salad recipe step 5.
6. Follow pasta recipe steps 5 through 9, and serve as first course.
7. Follow veal recipe step 5 and salad recipe step 6.
8. Follow veal recipe step 6 and salad recipe step 7.
9. Follow veal recipe steps 7 and 8, and serve with salad.

RECIPES

Angel Hair Pasta with Onions and Pepper Strips

1 lemon
Small red onion
1 pound white or yellow onions
¼ cup olive oil, preferably imported
¾ teaspoon salt
¼ teaspoon freshly ground black pepper
Pinch of sugar
1 red bell pepper
2 ounces Parmesan cheese, preferably imported
½ pound angel hair pasta (capelli d'angelo) or capellini
2 to 4 tablespoons unsalted butter
2 tablespoons chopped fresh parsley

1. Wash lemon, dry, and cut in half lengthwise. With paring knife, remove peel from one half of lemon, avoiding white pith; reserve remaining half for another use.
2. Peel red onion; cut into thin slices, separate into rings, and set aside. Peel and quarter white or yellow onions; cut into thin slivers. You will have about ½ cup red onion and about 2 cups white or yellow onions.
3. Heat oil in flameproof casserole over low heat. Add lemon peel and sauté 2 minutes.
4. Stir in slivered onions, salt, pepper, and pinch of sugar. Raise heat to medium, cover the casserole, and simmer, stirring occasionally to prevent sticking, 20 to 30 minutes, or until onions are well browned.
5. Bring 3 quarts of water to a boil over high heat.
6. Wash and dry red bell pepper. Halve, core, and seed pepper, and cut into ⅛-inch-thick strips. Set aside. Grate Parmesan to measure ½ cup. Set aside.
7. Add pasta to boiling water and, after water returns to a boil, cook about 30 seconds for angel hair pasta or 2 to 3 minutes for capellini. Turn pasta into colander to drain.
8. Add pasta to onions in casserole and toss gently.
9. Add red onion rings, pepper strips, butter to taste, parsley, and ¼ cup grated Parmesan to pasta, and toss. Divide pasta among bowls and serve with remaining Parmesan.

Veal Scallopini Marsala

2 tablespoons vegetable oil or light olive oil
¼ cup all-purpose flour, approximately
8 veal scallops (about 1¼ pounds total weight), pounded ¼ inch thick
4 tablespoons unsalted butter
½ cup sweet Marsala
2 tablespoons chopped parsley

1. Preheat oven to 200 degrees.
2. Heat oil in large heavy-gauge skillet over medium-high heat.
3. Meanwhile, place flour in pie pan or shallow dish. One by one, dust each scallop very lightly with flour, place in skillet, and sauté about 1 minute per side. Do *not* overcrowd skillet; cook scallops in 2 batches, if necessary.
4. As they are cooked, transfer scallops to heatproof platter and keep warm in oven; wipe out skillet.
5. Place 4 dinner plates in oven to warm.
6. Add butter and Marsala to skillet and bring to a boil over high heat; continue boiling 2 to 3 minutes, or until slightly thickened.
7. Reduce heat to low. Return scallops to pan and, using tongs, turn scallops several times until well coated.
8. Divide scallops among warm plates and sprinkle each serving with parsley.

Warm Vegetable Salad

1 pint cherry tomatoes
½ pound summer squash, if available
½ pound zucchini, or 1 pound, if not using summer squash
½ pound carrots
Large clove garlic
½ cup olive oil, preferably imported
2 to 3 tablespoons chopped fresh basil, or 2 to 3 teaspoons dried
Pinch of sugar
1 teaspoon salt
½ teaspoon freshly ground black pepper
2 tablespoons red wine vinegar, preferably imported

1. In medium-size saucepan fitted with vegetable steamer, bring to a boil enough water to come just up to but not above bottom of steamer.
2. Meanwhile, wash and dry tomatoes, summer squash, and zucchini. Remove stems from tomatoes. Trim off ends of summer squash and zucchini and discard. Cut into ¾-inch-thick rounds. Peel carrots, cut into 1½-inch-long pieces, and cut each piece lengthwise into quarters. You will have about 1¾ cups summer squash, 2 cups zucchini, and about 1 cup carrots. Peel garlic.
3. Place squash and zucchini in steamer; steam 2 minutes.
4. Transfer squash to large heatproof bowl. Place carrots in steamer and steam 10 minutes.
5. Add carrots to squash, cover and keep warm in oven.
6. Combine oil, basil, pinch of sugar, salt, and pepper in small saucepan. Put garlic through press, add to mixture

in pan, and cook over low heat 4 minutes.
7. Stir in vinegar and pour warm dressing over vegetables. Add whole cherry tomatoes and toss to combine.

ADDED TOUCH

For this creamy ricotta pudding, use imported Italian candied citrus peel if possible. If peel is unavailable, increase the mixture of dark and golden raisins and currants proportionately.

Ricotta Pudding

2 tablespoons candied citrus peel
1 tablespoon dark raisins
1 tablespoon golden raisins
1 tablespoon currants
¼ cup brandy or fruit-flavored liqueur
4 large eggs, at room temperature, separated
⅓ cup granulated sugar
1½ pounds ricotta or cottage cheese
Grated peel of 1 lemon
½ teaspoon vanilla extract
2 tablespoons all-purpose flour
Salt
1 tablespoon unsalted butter, approximately
¼ cup dried bread crumbs, approximately
Confectioners' sugar

1. Preheat oven to 350 degrees.
2. Chop candied citrus peel and combine with raisins, currants, and brandy in small bowl. Set aside to soak at least 15 minutes.
3. If using food processor, combine egg yolks, sugar, cheese, lemon peel, and vanilla, and process until combined. Add flour and process until blended. If using electric mixer, first combine yolks and sugar, and beat until thoroughly blended before adding cheese, flavorings, and flour.
4. Add brandy but not fruit to the mixture and blend; then add the fruit and blend briefly to combine.
5. Beat egg whites with a pinch of salt until stiff. Pour one third of cheese mixture over egg whites and gently fold in until almost incorporated. Add remaining cheese mixture and fold in until totally incorporated.
6. Generously butter 1½-quart soufflé dish. Add bread crumbs and evenly coat dish.
7. Turn pudding into prepared dish and place in baking pan. Fill pan with enough hot water to come halfway up sides of soufflé dish and bake 60 to 70 minutes, or until pudding is nicely browned.
8. Remove pudding from oven and let stand in water bath 30 minutes before unmolding.
9. To unmold, run thin-bladed knife around edge of soufflé dish. Place large flat plate upside down over dish and, holding plate and dish firmly together, turn upside down. If pudding does not unmold, rap plate and dish once against hard surface. Remove soufflé dish.
10. Sprinkle pudding with confectioners' sugar and serve.

Evelyne Slomon

Evelyne Slomon believes in pizza. "When made with cheese, vegetables, and perhaps some meat on a homemade crust, pizza is a nutritionally complete meal," she says. It requires no special equipment—only an oven, a bowl, and a flat baking sheet—and can be assembled in no time using a food processor to knead the dough. Even if you prepare the dough by hand, it does not take long (for details on making pizza dough by hand, see page 12).

In Italy, pizza varies markedly from one region to another. Evelyne Slomon's three menus demonstrate the adaptability of this dish. The home-style pizza of Menu 1 is known in Lombardy as *fitascetta*. This ring-shaped flat bread is usually topped with onions, but here it is covered with cheese and sautéed strips of red, yellow, and green pepper. *Fitascetta* is normally served as a bread, not as a main course, so the cook has added an antipasto platter and a soup to the meal.

Menu 2 offers the doughy deep-dish Sicilian pizza called *scacciata*, which is excellent hot or cold. This substantial pie, typical of the earthy fare of Sicily, has a thick, chewy crust and a topping of sautéed eggplant, anchovies, tomatoes, cheese, and olives. It is accompanied by two salads: one of escarole, chicory, and radicchio, and the other made with fennel and orange slices sweetened and dusted with cinnamon.

Neapolitan *calzoni*, or individual pizza turnovers enclosing a savory filling, are the main course of Menu 3. The cook uses an herb-seasoned blend of three cheeses to fill the *calzoni*, and serves them with stuffed eggplant fans and a tossed salad.

Topped with cheese and bell pepper strips, the pizza ring is good served hot or at room temperature. Offer it with a tureen of richly textured vegetable soup and a colorful antipasto platter.

Antipasto
Hearty Vegetable Soup
Home-style Pizza with Peppers

The antipasto can be prepared several hours in advance, covered with plastic wrap, and refrigerated. If you do so, remove the antipasto from the refrigerator 20 minutes before serving to bring it to room temperature.

To vary the pizza ring, use any combination of bell peppers you wish, and substitute some other mild cheese for the Fontina. Or fill the pizza sandwich-style: Split the ring in half, place a layer of arugula or lettuce leaves on the bottom ring, and top with slices of salami and a layer of sliced tomatoes. Drizzle a mild vinaigrette over the filling, replace the top ring, and cut the pizza into wedges. As a substitute for the spinach in the soup, try broccoli rabe, dandelion greens, escarole, or Swiss chard.

WHAT TO DRINK

A fruity red Dolcetto or Barbera is an excellent choice with this menu.

SHOPPING LIST AND STAPLES

¼ pound thinly sliced Genoa salami or other good-quality salami
2 ounces pancetta, prosciutto, or bacon
1 pound spinach
1 pint cherry tomatoes
3 small bell peppers, preferably 1 green, 1 red, and 1 yellow
Medium-size onion
Small bunch fresh parsley
2 cloves garlic, approximately
1 cup chicken stock, preferably homemade (see page 13), or canned
½ pound Italian Fontina cheese or other mild cheese
¼ pound Bel Paese cheese or other mild cheese
2 ounces Parmesan cheese, preferably imported
28-ounce can whole plum tomatoes
15-ounce can cannellini or other white or red beans
¼ cup plus 3 tablespoons olive oil
1 tablespoon vegetable oil, approximately
12-ounce jar medium-hot pickled peppers
7½-ounce jar oil-cured black olives or other Mediterranean olives
3½ cups all-purpose flour, preferably unbleached, approximately
1 package active dry yeast
Salt and freshly ground black pepper

UTENSILS

Food processor or blender
Large skillet with cover
Large heavy-gauge saucepan with cover
15-inch round pizza pan or 17 x 11-inch cookie sheet
Strainer
Measuring cups and spoons
Chef's knife
Serrated bread knife or pizza wheel
Paring knife
2 wooden spoons or spatulas
Grater (if not using processor)

START-TO-FINISH STEPS

1. Follow antipasto recipe steps 1 through 7.
2. Follow pizza recipe steps 1 through 8.
3. Follow soup recipe steps 1 through 4.
4. Follow pizza recipe steps 9 through 11.
5. Follow soup recipe steps 5 and 6.
6. Follow pizza recipe step 12 and soup recipe step 7.
7. While pizza is baking and soup is simmering, serve antipasto.
8. Follow soup recipe step 8 and serve with pizza.

RECIPES

Antipasto

12-ounce jar medium-hot pickled peppers
¼ pound Bel Paese cheese or other mild cheese
¼ pound thinly sliced Genoa salami or other good-quality salami
1 pint cherry tomatoes
6 sprigs parsley for garnish
2 dozen oil-cured black olives or other Mediterranean olives

1. Drain pickled peppers. Slit each pepper open by inserting point of paring knife ¼ inch below stem and cutting lengthwise down through tip. Remove seeds with tip of knife and discard.
2. Cut cheese into 2-inch-long by ¼-inch-thick pieces. Insert 1 piece of cheese into each pepper.
3. Overlap salami along outer edge of serving platter.
4. Arrange stuffed peppers over salami slices with tips facing outward.

5. Wash cherry tomatoes and dry with paper towels, leaving stems on if desired. Place tomatoes in center of platter.
6. Rinse parsley and dry with paper towels.
7. Scatter olives over platter and garnish with parsley.

Hearty Vegetable Soup

1 pound spinach
Medium-size onion
1 or 2 cloves garlic
2 ounces pancetta, prosciutto, or bacon
2 ounces Parmesan cheese
28-ounce can whole plum tomatoes
15-ounce can cannellini or other white or red beans
¼ cup olive oil
1 cup chicken stock
Salt and freshly ground pepper

1. Wash spinach thoroughly in several changes of cold water. Remove tough stems and discard. Coarsely chop spinach to make about 4 cups.
2. Peel and chop onion. Peel and finely mince 1 or 2 cloves garlic, according to taste. Cut pancetta into ½-inch cubes.
3. Using food processor or grater, grate Parmesan to make ½ cup; set aside.
4. Purée tomatoes with their juice in two batches in food processor or blender. Turn beans into strainer and rinse under cold running water; set aside.
5. Heat oil in large heavy-gauge saucepan over medium-high heat. Add onion and pancetta, and sauté 2 to 3 minutes, or until onion wilts and pancetta begins to brown.
6. Stir in spinach and garlic. Raise heat to high and cook, stirring, until spinach is wilted, about 2 minutes.
7. Add puréed tomatoes, beans, and stock, and bring to a boil. Lower heat and simmer, stirring occasionally, 10 to 15 minutes.
8. Add salt and pepper to taste and turn soup into tureen. Top with a generous spoonful of Parmesan and serve with remaining cheese.

Home-style Pizza with Peppers

1 package active dry yeast
3½ cups all-purpose flour, preferably unbleached, approximately
Salt
1 tablespoon vegetable oil, approximately
3 small bell peppers, preferably 1 green, 1 red, and 1 yellow
3 tablespoons olive oil
½ pound Italian Fontina cheese or other mild cheese
Freshly ground black pepper

1. Preheat oven to 450 degrees.
2. If not using food processor, prepare dough by hand (see page 12) and then proceed to step 4. If using processor, fit with dough blade or steel blade and pour in 1 cup hot tap water. Sprinkle in yeast and pulse machine on and off once or twice to dissolve yeast.
3. With processor running, add 3 cups flour, and ½ teaspoon salt; continue to process 10 to 15 seconds, or until

dough forms a ball. (With the steel blade, the dough often does not form a ball but forms a layer under or over the blade. This is fine.) Test consistency of dough by squeezing a small portion in your hand. If it sticks, add a bit more flour and process until no longer sticky; if dough is dry, add water, 1 tablespoon at a time, and process until smooth and elastic. Let dough rise in processor bowl 10 minutes.
4. Meanwhile, grease pizza pan or cookie sheet with vegetable oil and set aside.
5. Wash peppers and dry with paper towels. Halve, core, and seed peppers; cut into ¼-inch-thick strips.
6. Heat olive oil in large skillet over high heat. Add peppers and cook, covered, 3 to 4 minutes, stirring occasionally to prevent sticking.
7. Meanwhile, cut cheese into ⅛-inch-thick slices.
8. Remove peppers from heat and season with salt and pepper to taste; set aside.
9. Transfer dough to lightly floured work surface and knead briefly. Shape into 12-inch circle, pressing down with your fingertips. Push your fist down into center of circle to form 4-inch hole (like a large doughnut).
10. Transfer dough ring to prepared pan and reshape it if necessary.
11. Cover dough with cheese slices, top with peppers and their accumulated liquid, and let stand in a warm place 5 minutes.
12. Bake 15 to 20 minutes, or until golden and crusty.

This refreshing, creamy sherbet mixes quickly and does not require an ice-cream maker. You can substitute lime, orange, or grapefruit juice for the lemon juice and, if fresh raspberries are out of season, use whole frozen berries packed in heavy syrup.

Lemon Sorbetto with Raspberries

¾ cup freshly squeezed lemon juice
¾ cup superfine sugar
¾ cup heavy cream
1 cup fresh raspberries or whole frozen raspberries in heavy syrup
4 sprigs fresh mint for garnish (optional)
4 tablespoons Sambuca

1. Combine lemon juice and sugar in medium-size mixing bowl and stir until sugar is completely dissolved.
2. Stir in heavy cream.
3. Pour mixture into metal ice-cube tray (without sections) and freeze about 6 hours, or until solid.
4. One or two hours before serving, divide sherbet among individual bowls and return to freezer until ready to serve.
5. If using fresh raspberries, rinse gently in cold water and pat dry with paper towels.
6. Wash mint, if using, and dry.
7. Just before serving, remove sherbet from freezer. Top each serving with berries, drizzle with Sambuca, and garnish with a mint sprig, if desired.

Sicilian Pizza
Escarole, Chicory, and Radicchio Salad
Fresh Fennel and Oranges

For a family-style meal, serve a wedge of deep-dish pizza, a tossed salad, and sliced fennel and oranges.

When you make pizza, you learn that there are no hard and fast rules for what to use as a topping or filling. In this recipe, you can vary the topping by substituting two or three slices of fresh Italian sweet or hot sausages for the anchovies and capers. Use Provolone instead of *caciocavallo* cheese, or substitute chunks of zucchini for the eggplant. You can also season this pizza with oregano, fresh mint, and thyme.

The refreshing slices of raw fennel and orange sections are garnished with *pignoli*, or pine nuts. These slender, cream-colored nuts are popular throughout Italy in sweet and savory dishes. They come from a variety of Mediterra-

nean pine tree and have a delicate flavor. Because they turn rancid quickly, refrigerate any unused nuts in an airtight container. Pine nuts are sold in gourmet shops, health food stores, and many supermarkets. Use toasted almonds as a substitute, if necessary.

WHAT TO DRINK

To match the flavors of this meal, serve your guests a good dry red Sicilian wine such as Corvo Rosso or Etna Rosso. A good California Gamay is a fine domestic alternative.

Small eggplant (about 1 pound)
1 pound fresh tomatoes, or 28-ounce can whole tomatoes
Small head chicory
Small head escarole
Small head radicchio
Large fennel bulb with leaves, or small bunch celery
3 cloves garlic
2 small bunches parsley, or small bunch parsley plus
    small bunch basil
Medium-size lemon
4 large navel oranges
Medium-size juice orange
¾ pound mozzarella cheese
2 ounces caciocavallo or imported Provolone cheese
2-ounce tin anchovies
¾ cup olive oil, approximately
1 tablespoon vegetable oil, approximately
2 tablespoons red wine vinegar
2-ounce jar capers
7½-ounce jar oil-cured black olives
3½ cups all-purpose flour, approximately
2 tablespoons sugar or honey
1 package active dry yeast
2-ounce jar pignoli (pine nuts)
Small hot dried chili pepper
Pinch of cinnamon
Salt and freshly ground black pepper

UTENSILS

Food processor (optional)
Large skillet
15-inch round pizza pan, or 17 x 11-inch jelly-roll pan
13 x 9-inch cookie sheet
Large salad bowl
Medium-size bowl
2 small bowls
Salad spinner (optional)
Strainer
Measuring cups and spoons
Chef's knife
Serrated bread knife or pizza wheel
Paring knife
Wooden spoon
Spatula
Juicer (optional)
Grater (if not using processor)
Rolling pin

START-TO-FINISH STEPS

1. Wash and dry parsley and basil, if using. Mince enough parsley to measure 2 tablespoons for pizza recipe and enough parsley or basil to measure 2 tablespoons for escarole salad recipe. Peel garlic; mince 2 cloves for pizza recipe and crush 1 clove for escarole salad recipe.
2. Follow pizza recipe steps 1 through 11.

3. While pizza is baking, follow fennel and oranges recipe steps 1 through 7.
4. Follow pizza recipe step 12.
5. Follow escarole salad recipe step 1 and remove pizza from oven.
6. Follow escarole salad recipe steps 2 and 3, and serve with pizza and fennel and oranges.

RECIPES

Sicilian Pizza

1 package active dry yeast
½ cup olive oil
3½ cups all-purpose flour, approximately
Salt
1 tablespoon vegetable oil, approximately
Small hot dried chili pepper
Small eggplant (about 1 pound)
2-ounce tin anchovies
2 tablespoons capers
1 pound fresh tomatoes, or 28-ounce can whole tomatoes
2 cloves garlic, peeled and minced
2 tablespoons minced parsley
2 ounces caciocavallo or imported Provolone cheese
¾ pound mozzarella cheese
5 oil-cured black olives

1. Preheat oven to 450 degrees.
2. If not using food processor, prepare dough by hand (see page 12) and proceed to step 4. If using processor, fit with dough blade or steel blade and pour in ¾ cup hot tap water. Sprinkle in yeast and pulse machine on and off once or twice to dissolve the yeast.
3. With processor running, add ¼ cup olive oil, 3 cups flour, and ¼ teaspoon salt, and continue to process until dough forms a ball. (With the steel blade, the dough often does not form a ball but forms a layer under or over the blade. This is fine.) Test consistency of dough by squeezing a small portion in your hand. If it sticks to your palm, add a bit more flour and process until no longer sticky; if dough is dry, add water, 1 tablespoon at a time, and process until smooth and elastic.
4. Grease pizza or jelly-roll pan with vegetable oil and press dough over bottom and up 1 inch of sides with your fingertips. Or, you can use a rolling pin to roll dough out on a lightly floured surface and then fit it into pan in same manner, pressing 1 inch of dough up sides. Let dough rise in pan while you prepare filling.
5. Prepare dried chili pepper: Place pepper between 2 sheets of waxed paper and, using a rolling pin, bruise pepper for a spicy flavor, or pulverize it if you like a fiery taste.
6. Trim, peel, and coarsely chop eggplant into ½-inch dice to make 4 cups. Drain anchovies and capers.
7. Heat remaining ¼ cup olive oil in large skillet over medium heat. Add eggplant, season with chili pepper and salt to taste, and cook, stirring occasionally to prevent sticking, 5 minutes.

8. Meanwhile, if using fresh tomatoes, core, halve, seed, and coarsely chop to measure about 2 cups. If using canned tomatoes, drain and coarsely chop.

9. Add garlic and parsley to skillet and cook another 2 to 3 minutes, or until eggplant is tender.

10. Meanwhile, using food processor or grater, grate caciocavallo cheese to make ½ cup. Cut mozzarella into ¼-inch-thick slices; set aside.

11. Spread eggplant over dough and top with 1 layer each of anchovies, capers, tomatoes, caciocavallo cheese, and olives. Bake 20 minutes, or just until dough is golden.

12. Top with mozzarella and bake another 5 minutes, or until cheese is melted and bubbly. Cut into wedges or slices and serve.

Escarole, Chicory, and Radicchio Salad

Small head escarole
Small head chicory
Small head radicchio
2 tablespoons minced parsley or basil, or combination of both
2 tablespoons red wine vinegar
1 clove garlic, peeled and crushed
Salt and freshly ground black pepper
¼ cup olive oil, approximately

1. Wash escarole, chicory, and radicchio and discard bruised or discolored leaves. Dry in salad spinner or with paper towels. Combine greens, radicchio, and herbs in large salad bowl, cover with plastic wrap, and refrigerate until ready to serve.

2. Combine vinegar, garlic, and salt and pepper to taste in small bowl; beat with fork until salt dissolves. While beating with fork, add olive oil in a slow, steady stream and continue beating until dressing thickens.

3. Pour dressing over salad and toss until evenly coated. Divide among 4 dinner plates and serve.

Radicchio

Fresh Fennel and Oranges

¼ cup pignoli (pine nuts)
4 large navel oranges
Large fennel bulb with leaves, or small bunch celery
Medium-size juice orange
Medium-size lemon
2 tablespoons sugar or honey
Pinch of cinnamon

1. Place pignoli on cookie sheet and toast in 450-degree oven, shaking pan once or twice to prevent scorching, 3 to 5 minutes, or until golden.

2. Remove pignoli from oven and set aside to cool.

3. Using sharp paring knife, peel navel oranges over small bowl to catch juice. Reserve juice for dressing. Remove all traces of pith. Cut oranges crosswise into very thin rounds and set aside.

4. Trim off tops and bottom of fennel and cut bulb crosswise into thin slices. Reserve top leaves for garnish, if desired.

5. Squeeze enough juice from remaining orange to measure ¼ cup when combined with reserved juice in bowl. Juice lemon.

6. In medium-size bowl, combine orange and lemon juice with sugar and cinnamon to taste, and stir to combine. Add fennel slices and toss until well coated.

7. Divide orange slices among dinner plates. Top orange slices with fennel, sprinkle with toasted pignoli, and garnish with fennel leaves, if using, and a light dusting of cinnamon. Set aside until ready to serve.

ADDED TOUCH

This vegetable salad goes well not only with pizza but also with roasted or grilled chicken. Or, by adding blanched carrots, zucchini, green beans, and thinly sliced raw onions, you can expand this salad into a main course.

Sicilian Vegetable Salad

Small head broccoli (about 1 pound)
Small head cauliflower (about 1 pound)
Large red bell pepper
Small bunch parsley or basil (optional)
Medium-size lemon
2-ounce tin anchovies
1½ tablespoons capers
1 clove garlic
3½-ounce can imported oil-packed tuna
½ cup olive oil

1. Bring 3 quarts lightly salted water to a boil in large saucepan or stockpot over medium-high heat.

2. Meanwhile, trim broccoli and cauliflower, and cut into florets. Rinse bell pepper and dry. Core, halve, and seed pepper; cut into ¼-inch-thick slices. Wash parsley or basil, if using, dry with paper towels, and chop enough to measure 2 tablespoons. Juice lemon. Drain anchovies and capers.

3. Peel garlic and chop in food processor fitted with steel blade or in blender. Add half the anchovies, reserving remainder for another use. Add capers, tuna, tuna oil, lemon juice, and olive oil, and process until smooth.

4. Add broccoli and cauliflower to boiling water and blanch 3 to 5 minutes, or just until crisp-tender.

5. Transfer broccoli and cauliflower to colander, refresh under cold running water, and drain.

6. Arrange the broccoli, cauliflower, and pepper slices in large shallow bowl. Pour dressing over vegetables and garnish with chopped parsley or basil, if desired.

Calzoni with Three Cheeses
Stuffed Eggplant Fans
Arugula and Leaf Lettuce Salad

A basket of calzoni, *eggplant fans with sausage and tomato stuffing, and a green salad are perfect buffet fare.*

For the eggplant fans, select eggplants that are firm and shiny with fresh green tops. Baby eggplants have fewer seeds than mature ones, are less likely to be bitter, and need not be pared. To retain the eggplants' moisture, wrap them unwashed in a plastic bag and refrigerate until ready to use.

Goat cheese provides a tangy contrast to the bland mozzarella and ricotta in the filling for the *calzoni*. Young goat cheese is creamy and melts easily. Look for Italian *caprini di capra,* French log-shaped Montrachet (without the ash coating), Bûcheron, or a mild domestic goat cheese with herbs.

WHAT TO DRINK

A crisp white Vernaccia, a soft red Dolcetto, or a simple Sienese Chianti would go well with *calzoni.*

SHOPPING LIST AND STAPLES

4 Italian-style sweet sausages (about ¾ pound total weight)
4 small eggplants (about ¼ pound each)
4 small tomatoes (about 1 pound total weight)
Small head leaf lettuce
Small bunch arugula
Small yellow bell pepper
Medium-size sweet white onion
Small sweet red onion
Small bunch each fresh parsley, chives, and basil, or small bunch of any one of these
Small bunch fresh marjoram or oregano, or 1 teaspoon dried
2 cloves garlic
½ pound mozzarella cheese
½ pound ricotta
½ pound herbed goat cheese
3-ounce can walnut pieces
1¼ cups olive oil
1 tablespoon vegetable oil, approximately
2 tablespoons balsamic vinegar
3½ cups all-purpose flour, approximately
1 package active dry yeast
Salt
Coarsely ground black pepper

UTENSILS

Food processor (optional)
Two 17 x 11-inch baking pans
9 x 17-inch baking sheet (optional)
Large bowl
Medium-size bowl
Small bowl
Salad spinner (optional)
Measuring cups and spoons
Chef's knife
Paring knife
Wide metal spatula
Pastry brush
Rolling pin
Grater

START-TO-FINISH STEPS

1. Wash fresh herbs and pat dry. Chop enough parsley, basil, and chives to measure 1 tablespoon each for calzoni recipe, or chop 3 tablespoons of any one of these herbs. If using parsley, reserve 4 sprigs for garnish for eggplant recipe. If using fresh marjoram or oregano, mince enough to measure 2 teaspoons for eggplant recipe.
2. Follow calzoni recipe steps 1 through 3.
3. Follow eggplant recipe steps 1 through 7.
4. While eggplants are baking, follow calzoni recipe steps 4 through 11.
5. Follow salad recipe steps 1 through 4.
6. Follow eggplant recipe step 8.
7. Follow salad recipe steps 5 through 7 and serve with calzoni and eggplant.

RECIPES

Calzoni with Three Cheeses

1 package active dry yeast
3½ cups all-purpose flour, approximately
½ teaspoon salt
1 teaspoon coarsely ground black pepper
1 tablespoon vegetable oil, approximately
2 cloves garlic
½ pound mozzarella cheese
½ pound herbed goat cheese
½ pound ricotta
1 tablespoon each of minced fresh parsley, chives, and basil, or 3 tablespoons of any one of these
½ cup olive oil

1. Preheat oven to 500 degrees.
2. If not using food processor, prepare dough by hand (see page 12) and proceed to step 4. If using processor, fit with dough blade or steel blade and pour in 1 cup hot tap water. Sprinkle in yeast and pulse machine on and off once or twice to dissolve yeast.
3. With processor running, add 3 cups flour and the salt and pepper, and continue to process 10 to 15 seconds, or until dough forms a ball. (With the steel blade, the dough often does not form a ball but forms a layer under or over the blade. This is fine.) Test consistency of dough by squeezing a small portion of it in your hand. If it sticks to your palm, add a bit more flour and process until no longer sticky; if dough is dry, add water, 1 tablespoon at a time, and process until smooth and elastic. Let dough rise in processor bowl 10 minutes.
4. Grease large baking pan with vegetable oil.
5. Peel and mince garlic.
6. Using grater, coarsely shred mozzarella; crumble goat cheese by hand.

7. In medium-size mixing bowl, combine ricotta and goat cheese and blend with fork. Fold in garlic and herbs, being careful not to overmix or herbs will impart a greenish tinge. Fold in mozzarella.

8. Transfer dough to lightly floured work surface and knead briefly. Pat into ball and divide into quarters.

9. Using rolling pin and dusting with flour, if necessary, roll out each piece of dough into an 8-inch circle about ⅛ inch thick.

10. Place one fourth of filling on lower half of each circle, leaving a 1-inch border. Brush edges of dough with cold water and fold top half of circle over filling. Then fold border back to double seal, and crimp edges with tines of fork or with your fingers.

11. Using wide metal spatula, transfer calzoni to prepared baking pan. Brush with olive oil and bake on bottom rack of oven about 15 minutes, or until puffed and golden.

Stuffed Eggplant Fans

4 small eggplants (about ¼ pound each)
4 small tomatoes (about 1 pound total weight)
Medium-size sweet white onion
4 Italian-style sweet sausages (about ¾ pound total weight)
½ cup olive oil
2 teaspoons minced fresh marjoram or oregano, or 1 teaspoon dried
Salt and coarsely ground black pepper
4 parsley sprigs for garnish (optional)

1. Wash eggplants and dry with paper towels; do *not* trim off stem ends. Halve each eggplant lengthwise. With eggplant half cut-side down, make three lengthwise cuts, starting 1 inch below stem and slicing down through bottom. Repeat with remaining halves.

2. Wash tomatoes and dry with paper towels. Core and halve each tomato; cut each half into thirds.

3. Peel and quarter onion. Cut each quarter lengthwise into slivers.

4. Remove sausage meat from casings.

5. Grease large baking pan with 1 tablespoon oil and arrange eggplant fans cut-side down in a single layer.

6. Spread each fan open and stuff about 1 tablespoon sausage meat into each section. Cover meat with 1 tomato wedge and stuff any remaining spaces with onion slivers. Drizzle eggplant with remaining oil and sprinkle with marjoram or oregano, and salt and pepper to taste.

7. Place baking pan on top rack in 500-degree oven and bake eggplant 20 to 30 minutes, or just until tender. If fans begin to burn, cover loosely with foil and continue baking until tender.

8. With wide metal spatula, carefully transfer eggplant fans to serving platter and garnish with parsley, if desired.

Arugula and Leaf Lettuce Salad

½ cup walnut pieces
2 tablespoons balsamic vinegar
Salt and coarsely ground black pepper
¼ cup olive oil
Small bunch arugula
Small head leaf lettuce
Small yellow bell pepper
Small sweet red onion

1. Coarsely chop walnuts. Place on small baking sheet or on sheet of heavy-duty foil and roast in 500-degree oven 3 to 5 minutes, or until nicely browned.

2. While nuts are roasting, prepare dressing: Combine vinegar and salt and pepper to taste in small bowl, and stir with fork until salt dissolves. While beating with fork, add olive oil in a slow, steady stream and continue beating until dressing thickens slightly.

3. Stir hot walnuts into dressing and set aside.

4. Wash arugula and lettuce, and dry in salad spinner or with paper towels. Discard any wilted or bruised leaves; tear lettuce into bite-size pieces. Place greens in large bowl.

5. Wash bell pepper and dry. Halve, core, and seed pepper; cut into ¼-inch-thick strips.

6. Peel onion and slice thinly; separate into rings.

7. Just before serving, stir dressing to recombine, if necessary. Pour dressing over greens and toss until evenly coated. Top with pepper strips and onion rings.

ADDED TOUCH

Fresh or canned peaches steeped in red wine and topped with crumbled Italian macaroons are an easy dessert. For a delicious variation, serve the fruit over a generous portion of fresh *mascarpone*, a delicate, moist Italian cheese sometimes layered with Provolone or mixed with Gorgonzola.

Peaches in Red Wine

4 fresh sweet peaches, or 8 canned peach halves
Sugar
3 cups dry red wine
1 cup amaretti cookies or macaroons

1. If using macaroons, preheat oven to 350 degrees.

2. If using fresh peaches, wash under cold running water and dry with paper towels. Halve peaches and remove pits; do not peel. If using canned peaches, drain. Cut fresh or canned peaches into ½-inch-thick slices and place in serving bowl. If fresh peaches are not sweet enough, sprinkle with sugar to taste and toss gently until evenly coated.

3. Add wine to peaches. Set aside at room temperature for at least 4 hours, or cover with plastic wrap and refrigerate overnight.

4. Crumble amaretti or macaroons. If using macaroons, place crumbs on cookie sheet and toast 10 minutes, or until golden.

5. Remove macaroons from oven and set aside until ready to serve.

6. Divide peaches among individual bowls and sprinkle each serving with amaretti or macaroon crumbs.

Maggie Waldron

Maggie Waldron, who lived in Tuscany for a year, is an enthusiastic advocate of Italian cooking. "Even though this cuisine offers a broad spectrum of flavors," she says, "the Italians do not play tricks with food—a quality I love about them." Inspired by this direct approach to cooking, she presents three menus that have strong Italian overtones, yet are still very much her own.

The Menu 1 entrée pairs calf's liver and onions with an earthy risotto flavored with sage. A tart fruit salad of sliced oranges and lemons sprinkled with golden raisins and walnuts balances the main course.

For Menu 2 she serves angel hair pasta with chickpeas in a basil vinaigrette, a simple appetizer or main-course accompaniment. The sliced poached chicken breasts with homemade herb mayonnaise are arranged on a bed of watercress and radicchio and served with roasted artichokes and sliced lemons.

In Menu 3, fettuccine tossed with a creamy Cayenne-spiked sauce of Fontina and Parmesan cheeses, and pan-fried trout with fennel and bacon, make an impressive offering for guests. Fresh mozzarella and sun-dried tomatoes marinated in typical Italian seasonings—basil, garlic, olive oil, and anchovies—are the colorful salad.

Each helping of calf's liver is topped with crispy onion rings and presented with a portion of risotto. Offer the citrus salad on a separate plate and dress it just before serving.

Calf's Liver with Frizzled Onions
Sage Risotto
Orange and Lemon Salad

Top-quality calf's liver should smell fresh, look bright and moist, and be pinkish-brown. Do not buy beef liver, which has a dark red-brown color, feels firm rather than pliant, and has a beefy aroma. Many markets sell frozen liver, which is inferior to fresh liver. Calf's liver is best cooked rare—or just enough to lose its internal pink color. Lengthy cooking toughens the meat.

While a traditional creamy risotto is made with plump Italian Arborio rice, the cook uses long-grain rice here. With long-grain rice, each grain stays separate and fluffy when cooked.

Bitters adds a subtle sharpness to the salad dressing. Made from roots, bark, herbs, spices, and alcohol, bitters (such as Angostura or Fernet Branca) are sold in most supermarkets or liquor stores.

WHAT TO DRINK

A fruity red wine is the best match for these dishes. The cook suggests a California Gamay or a French Beaujolais.

SHOPPING LIST AND STAPLES

Four ½-inch-thick slices calf's liver (about 2 pounds total weight)
3 medium-size onions (about 1 pound total weight)
Large bunch watercress
Small bunch fresh parsley (optional)
Small bunch fresh sage, or 2½ teaspoons dried
2 navel oranges
3 large lemons, plus 1 large for garnish (optional)
3½ cups chicken stock, preferably homemade (see page 13), or two 13¾-ounce cans
6 tablespoons unsalted butter
2 tablespoons olive oil
⅔ cup vegetable oil, approximately
1 cup long-grain rice
12-ounce package golden raisins
3-ounce can walnut pieces
1½ teaspoons sugar
Salt and freshly ground black pepper
4-ounce bottle bitters

UTENSILS

Food processor or mandoline (optional)
Large heavy-gauge skillet
Medium-size heavy-gauge saucepan
Small saucepan
Large heavy-gauge sauté pan or Dutch oven
Platter
Small bowl
Measuring cups and spoons
Chef's knife
Paring knife
Wooden spoon
Slotted metal spoon
Small whisk
Metal tongs
Pastry brush

START-TO-FINISH STEPS

1. Squeeze enough lemon juice for liver and salad recipes. If using lemon garnish in liver recipe, wash, dry, and halve lemon and cut each half into quarters. Wash fresh sage, if using, dry with paper towels, and chop enough to measure 2 tablespoons for risotto; if desired, reserve 12 leaves for garnish for liver. Wash fresh parsley, if using, and chop enough to measure 2 tablespoons for risotto; if desired, reserve 4 sprigs for garnish for liver.
2. Follow salad recipe steps 1 through 4.
3. Follow risotto recipe steps 1 through 4.
4. Follow onions recipe step 1 and liver recipe steps 1 through 3.
5. Follow onions recipe steps 2 and 3, and liver recipe step 4.
6. Follow onions recipe step 4.
7. Follow salad recipe step 5, liver recipe steps 5 and 6, risotto recipe step 5, and serve.

RECIPES

Calf's Liver with Frizzled Onions

Four ½-inch-thick slices calf's liver (about 2 pounds total weight)
2 tablespoons lemon juice
Salt and freshly ground black pepper
2 tablespoons unsalted butter
2 tablespoons olive oil
Frizzled Onions (see following recipe)
1 large lemon, quartered for garnish (optional)
4 sprigs parsley for garnish (optional)
12 fresh sage leaves for garnish (optional)

1. Preheat oven to 200 degrees. Place 4 dinner plates in oven to warm.
2. Brush liver slices with lemon juice and sprinkle with salt and pepper to taste.
3. Combine butter and oil in large heavy-gauge skillet over high heat. Add liver and fry 4 to 5 minutes on one side, or until brown.
4. With metal tongs, turn liver and fry another 4 to 5 minutes on other side.
5. Divide liver among warm plates and top each serving with Frizzled Onions.
6. Just before serving, garnish each plate with lemon wedges, parsley, and sage leaves, if desired.

Frizzled Onions

2 medium-size onions (about ¾ pound total weight)
¼ cup vegetable oil
¼ teaspoon salt

1. Peel and halve onions. Using food processor fitted with slicing disk, or a mandoline or chef's knife, cut onions into *very* thin slices. You should have about 2½ cups. Dry onions with paper towels.
2. Line a platter with paper towels.
3. Heat oil in large heavy-gauge sauté pan or Dutch oven over high heat until just below smoking point. Add onions and cook, stirring frequently, until onions are dark brown and crisp, 5 to 8 minutes.
4. With slotted spoon, transfer to paper-towel-lined platter and sprinkle with salt.

Sage Risotto

Medium-size onion
4 tablespoons unsalted butter
1 cup long-grain rice
2 tablespoons chopped fresh sage leaves,
    or 2½ teaspoons dried
3½ cups chicken stock
2 tablespoons chopped fresh parsley (optional)

1. Peel onion and chop enough to measure ⅓ cup.
2. Melt butter in medium-size heavy-gauge saucepan over medium heat. Add onion and rice, and sauté, stirring frequently, 5 minutes. Do *not* brown.
3. Meanwhile, bring stock to a simmer in small saucepan over medium-high heat.
4. Add sage and 1 cup hot stock to rice mixture and bring

to a slow boil. Lower heat until mixture simmers gently and cook, stirring frequently, until liquid is absorbed, about 7 minutes. Repeat process twice more, using another 2 cups of hot stock. Test rice for texture. If liquid is absorbed before rice is cooked, add small amount of remaining hot stock and continue cooking just until rice is tender and liquid is absorbed. If rice is cooked before stock has been absorbed, raise heat to medium-high and boil off excess stock, being careful not to burn rice. Keep covered until ready to serve.
5. Divide risotto among dinner plates and sprinkle with parsley, if desired.

Sage

Orange and Lemon Salad

⅓ cup vegetable oil
¼ cup lemon juice
1½ teaspoons sugar
1 teaspoon bitters
½ teaspoon salt
⅛ teaspoon freshly ground black pepper
3 tablespoons golden raisins
Large bunch watercress
2 navel oranges
Large lemon
¼ cup walnut pieces

1. In small bowl, combine oil, lemon juice, sugar, bitters, salt, and pepper, and whisk until blended. Stir in raisins; set aside.
2. Wash watercress and dry with paper towels. Remove tough stems and discard. Divide among 4 individual salad plates.
3. With sharp paring knife, peel oranges and lemon, removing as much white pith as possible. Cut fruit crosswise into ⅛-inch-thick slices and divide among watercress-lined plates. Cover salads with plastic wrap and refrigerate.
4. Coarsely chop walnuts and set aside.
5. Just before serving, stir dressing to recombine. Drizzle salad with dressing and sprinkle with walnuts.

Angel Hair Pasta with Chickpeas
Italian Chicken Salad
Roasted Artichokes

Chicken salad with mayonnaise, artichoke flowers with lemon petals, and a light pasta are good hot-weather fare.

Select firm, compact artichokes with large fleshy leaves that close tightly around the central inedible choke. The stems should look moist and green. To store artichokes, wrap them unwashed in a damp towel, then in a plastic bag, and refrigerate them for up to five days. After trimming, rub all cut parts with lemon juice to prevent discoloration. Covering the artichokes with foil during roasting protects them from drying out and helps cook them quickly.

WHAT TO DRINK

Because a chemical component in artichokes sensitizes the taste buds, making wine (and food) taste sweeter, be sure to serve a well-chilled light, dry white wine. The cook's selection is a California Chenin Blanc, but you could also try an Italian Verdicchio or Pinot Grigio.

SHOPPING LIST AND STAPLES

2 skinless, boneless chicken breasts (about 1½ pounds total weight), halved
4 artichokes (about ½ pound each)
¾ pound greens, such as watercress, arugula, mustard greens, or dandelions
Small head radicchio (about ¼ pound)
1 bunch fresh cilantro
1 bunch fresh basil, or 1½ teaspoons dried
Large clove garlic
4 lemons
8-ounce can chickpeas
1 egg
1 cup olive oil, approximately
1 cup plus 2 teaspoons vegetable oil
⅓ cup white wine vinegar
2-ounce jar capers
½ pound angel hair pasta (capelli d'angelo)
Salt and freshly ground pepper
⅓ cup dry white wine

UTENSILS

Food processor or blender
Stockpot
Medium-size saucepan
Large bowl
Small bowl
4 ramekins or small custard cups
9-inch glass pie plate
Colander
Strainer
Measuring cups and spoons
Chef's knife
Paring knife
2 wooden spoons
Slotted spoon
Rubber spatula
Small whisk
Kitchen scissors
Pastry brush
Garlic press
Juicer

START-TO-FINISH STEPS

1. Wash cilantro, and fresh basil if using, and pat dry with paper towels. Remove stems from enough cilantro to measure ⅓ cup firmly packed sprigs; reserve 4 sprigs for garnish for chicken salad. Chop enough basil to measure 3 tablespoons for pasta recipe.
2. Follow artichokes recipe steps 1 through 4.
3. Follow pasta recipe steps 1 through 7.
4. Follow chicken salad recipe steps 1 through 6.
5. Follow artichokes recipe step 5 and pasta recipe step 8.
6. Follow chicken salad recipe steps 7 and 8, artichokes recipe step 6, and serve with pasta.

RECIPES

Angel Hair Pasta with Chickpeas

2 teaspoons salt
2 teaspoons vegetable oil
2 teaspoons capers
½ cup olive oil
⅓ cup white wine vinegar
¼ teaspoon freshly ground pepper
3 tablespoons coarsely chopped fresh basil, or 1½ teaspoons dried
½ pound angel hair pasta (capelli d'angelo)
8-ounce can chickpeas

1. Bring 2 quarts water, 1½ teaspoons salt, and vegetable oil to a boil in stockpot over high heat.
2. In strainer, drain capers.
3. For dressing, combine olive oil, vinegar, remaining ½ teaspoon salt, and pepper in small bowl, and whisk until well blended. Stir in basil and drained capers; set aside.
4. Add pasta to boiling water, return water to a boil, and cook according to package directions until just tender, about 5 minutes.
5. Meanwhile, turn chickpeas into strainer and rinse thoroughly under cold running water; set aside to drain.
6. Turn pasta into colander and drain; transfer to large bowl.
7. Add chickpeas and vinaigrette to pasta and toss to combine. Cover bowl with plastic wrap and set aside.
8. Just before serving, toss pasta to recombine. Divide among 4 individual salad plates and top each serving with any dressing left in bottom of bowl.

Italian Chicken Salad

2 skinless, boneless chicken breasts (about 1½ pounds total weight), halved
1¾ teaspoons salt
¾ pound greens, such as watercress, arugula, mustard greens, or dandelions

Small head radicchio (about ¼ pound)
2 lemons
1 egg
⅓ cup firmly packed cilantro sprigs, plus 4 sprigs for
    garnish (optional)
1 cup vegetable oil

1. Combine chicken breasts, 1 teaspoon salt, and enough water to cover in medium-size saucepan, and bring to a boil over medium heat. Reduce heat and gently simmer about 15 minutes, or until chicken is cooked through and juices run clear when meat is tested with tip of knife.
2. Meanwhile, wash greens and radicchio, and dry with paper towels. Remove any bruised or discolored leaves and discard. Wrap remaining greens and radicchio in paper towels and refrigerate.
3. Squeeze enough lemon to measure 3 tablespoons juice.
4. Prepare mayonnaise: In container of food processor or blender, combine egg, lemon juice, 2 tablespoons water, ¾ teaspoon salt, and ⅓ cup cilantro, and process until cilantro is finely chopped.
5. With machine running, add oil in slow, steady stream and process until mixture is thick and smooth.
6. With slotted spoon, remove chicken from pan and set aside to cool at least 10 minutes.
7. Divide radicchio among 4 individual dinner plates and top with greens. Cut each piece of chicken crosswise into 6 or 8 slices and place on greens. Top each serving with a spoonful of mayonnaise; divide remainder among 4 individual ramekins.
8. Place a ramekin on each plate and garnish with sprig of cilantro.

Roasted Artichokes

4 artichokes (about ½ pound each)
⅓ cup olive oil
⅓ cup dry white wine
Large clove garlic
2 lemons

1. Preheat oven to 450 degrees.
2. With sharp paring knife, cut off stems and about ½ inch from tops of artichokes. Wash artichokes thoroughly under cold running water and drain upside-down on double layer of paper towels.
3. In 9-inch glass pie plate, combine oil and wine. Peel garlic and put through press; add to oil and wine.

4. With scissors, snip off ¼ inch from tip of each leaf. Roll artichokes in oil mixture; then stand in pie plate, stem-ends down. Spoon oil mixture over artichokes, cover them tightly with heavy-duty foil, and roast 45 to 50 minutes, or until hearts are tender when pricked with toothpick and an outer leaf comes off easily when tugged.
5. Wash lemons and dry; cut each crosswise into approximately 12 very thin slices.
6. Remove artichokes from oven. Brush them with pan liquid, tuck about 6 lemon slices between leaves of each artichoke, and transfer to dinner plates.

ADDED TOUCH

Both the Italian amaretto liqueur and the crisp amaretti cookies add a subtle almond flavor to this delectable chocolate dessert. Be sure to chill in the refrigerator for at least 3 hours.

Chocolate Amaretto Cream

3 tablespoons granulated sugar
1 cup semi-sweet chocolate pieces
¼ cup amaretto liqueur
1¼ cups heavy cream
2 tablespoons crushed amaretti (Italian almond
    macaroons)

1. Place electric beaters and large bowl in freezer to chill. Combine sugar and 3 tablespoons water in small saucepan and bring to a boil, stirring, over medium heat. Continue to boil 1 minute.
2. Combine chocolate and sugar mixture in blender and blend until smooth, scraping down sides of container with rubber spatula as necessary. Add 3 tablespoons amaretto and blend until thoroughly incorporated; set aside.
3. In large bowl, beat 1 cup heavy cream with electric mixer at high speed until stiff.
4. With rubber spatula, fold chocolate mixture into whipped cream until totally incorporated. Cover bowl with plastic wrap and refrigerate at least 3 hours.
5. Just before serving, in small bowl, beat remaining ¼ cup heavy cream with electric mixer at high speed until it forms soft peaks. Add remaining tablespoon amaretto and beat until stiff.
6. Divide chocolate mixture among stemmed dessert glasses or bowls, top each serving with a spoonful of whipped cream, and sprinkle with amaretti crumbs.

Marinated Mozzarella with Sun-Dried Tomatoes and Anchovies
Trout with Fennel and Bacon
Fettuccine in Cayenne Cream Sauce

For a meal that pleases the eye as well as the palate, serve whole fried trout, a mozzarella salad, and a bowl of fettuccine.

Whole pan-fried trout is the main course for this festive meal. One of the most popular freshwater fish, trout is available either fresh or frozen in most supermarkets. Store fresh trout packed in ice until you are ready to cook it; defrost frozen trout overnight in the refrigerator. Fresh fennel is a primary component of the main course, and the cook says that there is no substitute. For information about fennel, see page 10.

WHAT TO DRINK

A full-bodied, slightly fruity white wine would be an excellent companion to this menu. Choose an Italian Gavi or

Pinot Bianco or, for a fine domestic alternative, a moderately priced California Chardonnay.

SHOPPING LIST AND STAPLES

4 small trout (each about ½ pound), scaled and gutted
4 thick slices bacon (about ¼ pound)
½ pound greens, such as dandelion, endive, or arugula
2 fennel bulbs with leaves (1½ to 2 pounds total weight)
Small red onion
Small bunch fresh parsley
1 bunch fresh basil, or 2 teaspoons dried
Large clove garlic

3 lemons
½ pint heavy cream
½ pound fresh mozzarella cheese, or 8-ounce package
   good-quality mozzarella
¼ pound Fontina cheese, preferably Italian
2 ounces Parmesan cheese, preferably imported
⅔ cup vegetable oil, approximately
⅓ cup olive oil
⅓ cup red wine vinegar
¼ pound oil-packed sun-dried tomatoes, or 4-ounce jar
   whole pimientos
2-ounce tin anchovy fillets
½ pound fettuccine
2 tablespoons all-purpose flour
1 teaspoon fennel seeds
Cayenne pepper
Salt
Freshly ground black pepper

UTENSILS

Food processor (optional)
Stockpot
2 large skillets, 1 with cover
Small nonaluminum saucepan
Medium-size bowl
Salad spinner (optional)
Colander
Strainer
Measuring cups and spoons
Chef's knife
Paring knife
2 wooden spoons
Slotted spoon
Wide metal spatula
Small whisk
Juicer (optional)
Grater (if not using processor)
Garlic press
Pastry brush

START-TO-FINISH STEPS

1. Wash fresh parsley, and fresh basil if using, and dry with paper towels. Chop enough parsley to measure ¼ cup for fettuccine recipe and enough basil to measure 1½ tablespoons for mozzarella recipe.
2. Follow mozzarella recipe steps 1 through 5.
3. Follow trout recipe steps 1 through 6.
4. Follow fettuccine recipe steps 1 through 4.
5. Follow trout recipe steps 7 through 9.
6. While trout is cooking, follow fettuccine recipe step 5 and mozzarella recipe step 6.
7. Follow trout recipe step 10 and fettuccine recipe steps 6 through 8.
8. Follow trout recipe steps 11 and 12, and serve with fettuccine and mozzarella.

RECIPES

Marinated Mozzarella with Sun-Dried Tomatoes and Anchovies

Large clove garlic
⅓ cup vegetable oil
⅓ cup olive oil
⅓ cup red wine vinegar
1½ tablespoons chopped fresh basil, or 2 teaspoons dried
½ teaspoon salt
¼ teaspoon freshly ground black pepper
½ pound fresh mozzarella cheese, or 8-ounce package
   good-quality mozzarella
½ pound greens, such as dandelion, endive, or arugula
Small red onion
½ cup oil-packed sun-dried tomatoes, or 4-ounce jar
   whole pimientos
2-ounce tin anchovy fillets

1. Peel garlic and put through press into medium-size bowl. Add vegetable and olive oils, vinegar, basil, salt, and pepper, and whisk until blended.
2. Cut mozzarella into ½-inch cubes. Add to dressing and toss until well coated. Cover bowl with plastic wrap and set aside 20 minutes to marinate.
3. Wash greens and dry in salad spinner or with paper towels. Remove any bruised or discolored leaves and discard. Line serving platter with greens.
4. Peel onion and cut into ⅛-inch-thick slices; separate into rings. Drain tomatoes or pimientos in strainer and cut into bite-size pieces. Drain anchovies.
5. Top greens with onion rings, tomatoes, and anchovies. Cover platter with plastic wrap and refrigerate until ready to serve.
6. Just before serving, spoon mozzarella into center of salad and drizzle with any dressing left in bottom of bowl.

Trout with Fennel and Bacon

4 thick slices bacon (about ¼ pound)
3 lemons
2 fennel bulbs with leaves (1½ to 2 pounds total weight)
1 teaspoon fennel seeds
Salt
Freshly ground black pepper
4 small trout (each about ½ pound), scaled and gutted
3 tablespoons vegetable oil
2 tablespoons all-purpose flour

1. Cut bacon into ½-inch pieces and fry in large skillet over medium heat, stirring occasionally, 7 to 8 minutes, or until lightly browned and crisp.
2. Meanwhile, rinse 1 lemon, dry, and cut crosswise into ¼-inch-thick rounds. Stack rounds and cut in half; set aside. Squeeze enough of remaining lemons to measure ¼ cup juice.
3. Rinse fennel under cold running water. Trim off ends and reserve feathery leaves. Cut bulbs diagonally into ¼-inch-thick slices and dry with paper towels.

4. Using slotted spoon, transfer bacon pieces to double thickness of paper towels to drain; reserve drippings in skillet.

5. Spoon half of reserved bacon fat into another large skillet and heat over high heat. Add sliced fennel and fennel seeds, and stir fry 5 minutes.

6. Sprinkle fennel with about half the lemon juice and season with salt and pepper to taste. Cover skillet and remove from heat.

7. Rinse trout under cold running water and dry gently with paper towels. Cut two 2-inch-long diagonal slits in each side of trout. Brush trout inside and out with remaining lemon juice and season with salt and pepper to taste.

8. Add oil to drippings in reserved skillet and heat over high heat.

9. Stuff cavities and slits in each trout with reserved fennel leaves. Lightly dust trout with flour. Place trout in skillet and cook on one side about 4 minutes, or just until skin is browned and flesh is opaque.

10. With wide metal spatula, turn fish and cook another 4 minutes on other side.

11. Return skillet with fennel to high heat and stir fry 2 minutes, or until heated through.

12. Transfer trout to platter, top with fennel and bacon, and garnish with lemon slices.

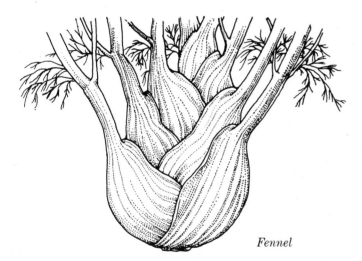

Fennel

Fettuccine in Cayenne Cream Sauce

1 cup heavy cream
¼ pound Fontina cheese, preferably Italian
2 ounces Parmesan cheese, preferably imported
Salt
1½ teaspoons vegetable oil
Cayenne pepper
½ pound fettuccine
¼ cup chopped parsley

1. Pour cream into small nonaluminum saucepan and bring to a boil over medium heat; immediately reduce heat to low, and simmer 5 minutes.

2. Meanwhile, using food processor or grater, finely shred enough Fontina to measure ½ to ¾ cup, and grate enough Parmesan to measure 3 tablespoons.

3. Bring 2 quarts water, 2 teaspoons salt, and oil to a boil in stockpot over high heat.

4. Reduce heat under cream to very low and gradually add cheeses, stirring constantly until cheeses are melted; do *not* boil. Stir in salt and Cayenne pepper to taste, cover, and set aside.

5. Add fettuccine to boiling water and stir to separate strands. Allow water to return to a boil and cook according to package directions, or until just tender, about 7 to 8 minutes.

6. Drain fettuccine in colander and return to pot.

7. Briefly reheat sauce, stirring, over low heat; do not allow to boil.

8. Add sauce and 2 tablespoons parsley to fettuccine and toss to combine. Turn fettuccine into serving bowl and sprinkle with remaining parsley.

ADDED TOUCH

For this cooling dessert, select only the freshest, ripest strawberries.

Strawberry Semifreddo

1½ pints strawberries
3 egg whites
1½ teaspoons vanilla extract
⅓ cup granulated sugar
¾ cup heavy cream
1 tablespoon confectioners' sugar
2 teaspoons lemon juice

1. Gently rinse strawberries and dry with paper towels. Hull berries and purée about 1 pint in food processor or blender; reserve remaining berries.

2. Combine purée, egg whites, and 1 teaspoon vanilla in large bowl and beat with electric mixer until frothy and pale, about 2 minutes.

3. Add granulated sugar gradually to strawberry mixture, beating until totally incorporated.

4. In another bowl, beat heavy cream with electric mixer at high speed until it forms soft peaks. Fold cream into strawberry mixture, cover bowl, and chill in freezer 1 hour.

5. After 1 hour, remove mixture from freezer and beat with electric mixer until thoroughly blended. Cover, return to freezer, and chill until firm, about 3 hours.

6. Meanwhile, halve remaining strawberries. Combine them with remaining vanilla, confectioners' sugar, and lemon juice in medium-size bowl and toss gently to combine. Cover with plastic wrap and refrigerate until ready to serve.

7. About 10 to 15 minutes before serving, set out frozen strawberry mixture to soften at room temperature.

8. When somewhat softened, divide semifreddo among individual goblets or bowls and top each serving with sweetened strawberries.

Maria Luisa and Jack Denton Scott

J ack Denton Scott and his Italian wife, Maria Luisa, frequently serve pasta because of its many attributes. For instance, the first-course pasta of Menu 1—a slender variety called *fedelini*—is a neutral base for the highly spiced sauce (*salsa puttanesca*) reputedly devised by Neapolitan prostitutes who could quickly and easily prepare it between appointments. For the entrée, the Scotts offer poached whiting with clams in a broth (a recipe they discovered in the southern seacoast city of Bari) and an escarole salad from Florence.

While pasta is the perfect foil for strong flavors, it can easily stand on its own merits and be enjoyed for its delicate taste. In Menu 2, the cooks prepare spaghettini seasoned with butter, cream, and two varieties of grated cheese. With it they serve sausages in a peppery tomato sauce and braised romaine lettuce.

Although pasta is a national staple in Italy, it is by no means the only Italian starch. Menu 3, a mix of regional recipes, offers a saffron rice from Milan—rather than a pasta—as the base for broiled Florentine lamb kidneys. The side salad of oranges and Kalamata olives is reminiscent of Sicily.

Use large deep plates to accommodate each serving of whiting, clams, and broth, which should be presented after the pasta. Let your guests help themselves to salad and chunks of crusty warm Italian bread.

Pasta with Tomato, Anchovy, and Olive Sauce
Poached Whiting with Clams
Escarole and Gorgonzola Salad

Whiting is a delicately flavored fish that is both cheap and plentiful. If possible, buy the fish scaled and gutted, but with the heads and tails intact. Because whiting crumbles easily during cooking, handle it gently. Cherrystone clams, called quahogs in New England, are available year-round nationwide. Keep them in the refrigerator until ready to use; then scrub them with a stiff brush to remove any dirt.

WHAT TO DRINK

With this Southern Italian menu, serve a white Neapolitan wine such as Greco di Tufo or Lacryma Christi.

SHOPPING LIST AND STAPLES

4 small whiting, gutted and scaled (about ½ pound each)
2 dozen small cherrystone clams
2 heads escarole (about 2 pounds total weight)
Small bunch parsley
1 shallot
5 cloves garlic
2 lemons
28-ounce can plum tomatoes, preferably imported
4 tablespoons unsalted butter
¼ pound Gorgonzola cheese, preferably imported
½ cup plus 1 tablespoon olive oil
1 tablespoon tarragon vinegar
2-ounce tin rolled anchovies
11-ounce jar black olives, preferably Kalamata
4¾-ounce jar pimiento-stuffed green olives
¾ pound fedelini, preferably imported, or capellini or spaghettini
1 teaspoon dried oregano
¼ teaspoon red pepper flakes
½ teaspoon anise seeds
¼ teaspoon dry mustard
Salt
Coarse (kosher) salt
Freshly ground black pepper
8 black peppercorns
2 cups dry white wine, approximately

UTENSILS

Stockpot
Shallow ovenproof casserole or Dutch oven with cover
Large nonaluminum saucepan
Large salad bowl
3 small bowls
Colander
Strainer
Measuring cups and spoons
Chef's knife
Paring knife
2 wooden spoons
Metal spatula

START-TO-FINISH STEPS

1. Peel and mince shallot for pasta recipe; peel and mince garlic for pasta, fish, and salad recipes.
2. Follow pasta recipe steps 1 through 5.
3. While sauce is cooking, follow salad recipe steps 1 through 4 and pasta recipe step 6.
4. Follow fish recipe steps 1 through 3.
5. Follow pasta recipe steps 7 and 8, and fish recipe step 4.
6. Follow pasta recipe step 9 and fish recipe step 5.
7. While fish is cooking, follow pasta recipe steps 10 through 12 and serve.
8. Follow fish recipe steps 6 and 7.
9. Follow salad recipe step 5, fish recipe step 8, and serve.

RECIPES

Pasta with Tomato, Anchovy, and Olive Sauce

28-ounce can plum tomatoes, preferably imported
8 black olives, preferably Kalamata
8 pimiento-stuffed green olives
2-ounce tin rolled anchovies
4 tablespoons unsalted butter
1 clove garlic, peeled and minced
1 shallot, peeled and minced
¼ teaspoon red pepper flakes
1 teaspoon dried oregano
1 tablespoon salt
1 tablespoon olive oil
¾ pound fedelini, preferably imported, or capellini or spaghettini

1. Reserving liquid, finely chop tomatoes.
2. If necessary, remove pits from black olives. Slice black and green olives. Drain anchovies.

3. In large nonaluminum saucepan, heat 2 tablespoons butter over medium heat. Add minced garlic and shallot, and sauté, stirring occasionally, 3 minutes, or until soft. Do *not* brown.
4. Add anchovies and sauté, stirring occasionally, about 2 minutes, or until they disintegrate.
5. Stir in tomatoes, their liquid, olives, pepper flakes, and oregano, and simmer, stirring occasionally, about 20 minutes, or until sauce has thickened. Do *not* overcook.
6. Meanwhile, bring 3 quarts water, salt, and olive oil to a boil in stockpot over high heat.
7. Add pasta to boiling water and cook according to package directions until *al dente*. Avoid overcooking.
8. Check sauce; if slightly thickened, remove from heat and cover to keep warm.
9. Turn pasta into colander and drain.
10. Add remaining butter to stockpot. Return pasta to pot, and gently toss with 2 wooden spoons until coated.
11. Add about one third of the sauce to pasta and toss.
12. Divide pasta among bowls, top each serving with remaining sauce, and serve.

Poached Whiting with Clams

Small bunch parsley
2 cloves garlic, peeled and minced
2 lemons
4 small whiting, gutted and scaled (about ½ pound each)
¼ cup olive oil
Salt and freshly ground black pepper
2 cups dry white wine, approximately
2 dozen small cherrystone clams

1. Preheat oven to 350 degrees.
2. Wash parsley and dry with paper towels; chop enough to measure ⅓ cup. Combine parsley and garlic in small bowl and toss to combine.
3. Squeeze lemons to measure ¼ cup juice.
4. Evenly coat the fish with olive oil and place them, skin-side down, in shallow ovenproof casserole or Dutch oven just large enough to hold them snugly. Sprinkle with lemon juice, garlic-parsley mixture, and salt and pepper to taste. Add enough wine to fill casserole to a depth of ½ inch. Cover and bring to a simmer over medium-high heat.
5. Transfer casserole to oven and cook 20 minutes.
6. After whiting have cooked 20 minutes, remove clams from refrigerator and scrub thoroughly under cold running water.
7. Add clams to whiting, return to oven, and cook, uncovered, another 10 minutes, until fish flakes easily when tested with a fork and clams open.
8. With metal spatula, transfer fish to deep plates or to large bowls, top with clams and broth, and serve.

Escarole and Gorgonzola Salad

2 heads escarole (about 2 pounds total weight)
1 tablespoon tarragon vinegar
¼ teaspoon dry mustard
¼ cup olive oil
2 cloves garlic, peeled and minced
½ teaspoon anise seeds
Coarse (kosher) salt
8 black peppercorns
¼ pound Gorgonzola cheese, preferably imported

1. Wash and dry escarole. Discard any bruised or discolored leaves and wrap remaining leaves in paper towels and refrigerate.
2. In small bowl, combine vinegar and dry mustard, and beat with fork until blended. Add olive oil in slow, steady stream, beating continuously, until slightly thickened.
3. In another small bowl, combine garlic, anise seeds, salt to taste, and peppercorns, and crush with back of spoon. Add to dressing and stir with fork until blended; set aside.
4. Crumble Gorgonzola to make about 1 cup and set aside.
5. When ready to serve, place escarole in large salad bowl. If necessary, stir dressing to recombine. Pour over escarole and toss until coated. Top with Gorgonzola.

ADDED TOUCH

For this simple dessert, use a tart apple such as a Granny Smith, Northern Spy, or McIntosh.

Tuscan Tart

4-ounce can blanched almonds
2 tablespoons unsalted butter for pan
1½ cups granulated sugar
3 tablespoons all-purpose flour
1 tablespoon baking powder
¼ teaspoon salt
2 eggs
Large tart apple (about ¾ pound), coarsely chopped
1 teaspoon vanilla extract
½ pint heavy cream or soft vanilla ice cream

1. Preheat oven to 350 degrees.
2. Coarsely chop almonds. Place on 15 x 10-inch baking sheet and toast in oven, shaking pan occasionally to prevent scorching, 10 to 15 minutes, or until browned.
3. Butter bottom and sides of 9-inch springform pan.
4. Remove almonds from oven and set aside to cool.
5. Sift together sugar, flour, baking powder, and salt.
6. In large mixing bowl, beat eggs until light and lemony in color. Gradually add sifted dry ingredients, beating well after each addition, until totally incorporated.
7. Add apple, almonds, and vanilla to batter, and stir until well blended. Pour into prepared pan and bake 40 minutes, or until top is golden and crusty.
8. If using heavy cream, place electric beaters and bowl in freezer to chill.
9. Transfer tart to rack to cool 5 to 8 minutes.
10. While cake is cooling, whip heavy cream, if using, with electric mixer at high speed until stiff.
11. When pan is cool to the touch, remove ring. The tart will fall, which is fine.
12. Cut tart into slices and serve garnished with whipped cream or vanilla ice cream.

Sausages Pizzaiola
Spaghettini with Two Cheeses
Braised Romaine Lettuce

For variety and texture, cut the sausages into different lengths before adding them to the tomato sauce. The pasta is tossed with butter and cheese, then served with the sausages. Braised romaine lettuce is the vegetable side dish.

The tomato sauce for the sausages should be light and fresh, tasting predominantly of the tomatoes and not the seasonings. Because the acid in tomatoes reacts with certain metals (such as aluminum), be sure to cook this sauce in a stainless-steel, enamel, or other coated pot.

WHAT TO DRINK

A fruity red wine such as a top-quality Valpolicella, a good Dolcetto, or a domestic Zinfandel will accompany this menu admirably.

SHOPPING LIST AND STAPLES

4 sweet Italian sausages (about 1 pound total weight)
4 hot Italian sausages (about 1 pound total weight)
Large head romaine lettuce (about 2 pounds)
Small bunch fresh parsley
5 cloves garlic
3½ cups chicken stock, preferably homemade (see page 13), or two 13¾-ounce cans
28-ounce can Italian plum tomatoes, preferably imported
6 tablespoons unsalted butter
½ pint heavy cream
2 ounces Asiago cheese, preferably, or Parmesan
2 ounces pecorino Romano cheese
¼ cup plus 3 tablespoons olive oil
¾ to 1 pound spaghettini
1 teaspoon dried oregano
¼ teaspoon red pepper flakes
Salt and freshly ground black pepper

UTENSILS

Nonaluminum stockpot or Dutch oven
Large heavy-gauge skillet
Large saucepan
Medium-size sauté pan with cover
2 large bowls
Small bowl
Colander
Strainer
Food mill (optional)
Measuring cups and spoons
Chef's knife
Paring knife
2 wooden spoons

Slotted metal spoon
Grater

START-TO-FINISH STEPS

1. Follow sausages recipe steps 1 through 4.
2. While sauce simmers, follow lettuce recipe steps 1 and 2.
3. Follow sausages recipe step 5.
4. While sauce simmers, follow lettuce recipe steps 3 through 5 and spaghettini recipe steps 1 and 2.
5. Follow lettuce recipe step 6.
6. Follow sausages recipe step 6 and spaghettini recipe steps 3 through 6.
7. Follow sausages recipe step 7.
8. Follow spaghettini recipe step 7 and lettuce recipe step 7.
9. Follow spaghettini recipe step 8 and lettuce recipe steps 8 and 9.
10. Follow spaghettini recipe steps 9 and 10, sausages recipe step 8, and serve with lettuce.

RECIPES

Sausages Pizzaiola

28-ounce can Italian plum tomatoes, preferably imported
3 cloves garlic
2 tablespoons olive oil
1 teaspoon salt
¼ teaspoon red pepper flakes
1 teaspoon dried oregano
4 sweet Italian sausages (about 1 pound total weight)
4 hot Italian sausages (about 1 pound total weight)

1. Put tomatoes with their liquid through food mill held over large bowl, or chop finely with chef's knife and combine with liquid.
2. Crush garlic under flat blade of chef's knife; peel.
3. In large saucepan, heat olive oil over medium heat. Add garlic and sauté, stirring, 3 minutes; do *not* brown.
4. Add tomatoes with their liquid and simmer, uncovered, 10 minutes, stirring occasionally.
5. Stir in salt, red pepper flakes, and oregano, and simmer, uncovered, 15 minutes, stirring occasionally. Remove pan from heat and set aside.
6. Prick all sausages in several places with tip of sharp knife. Place sausages in large heavy-gauge skillet with enough water to cover and bring water to a boil over high heat. Lower heat and simmer sausages 10 to 15 minutes.
7. With slotted metal spoon, transfer sausages to pan with sauce. Bring to a simmer over medium heat and cook, stirring occasionally, 15 minutes.
8. When ready to serve, divide sausages among 4 dinner plates, spooning sauce over them.

Spaghettini with Two Cheeses

1 tablespoon salt
1 tablespoon olive oil
Small bunch fresh parsley
2 ounces Asiago cheese, preferably, or Parmesan
2 ounces pecorino Romano cheese
Freshly ground black pepper
¾ to 1 pound spaghettini
6 tablespoons unsalted butter
2 tablespoons heavy cream

1. Preheat oven to 200 degrees.
2. Bring 3 quarts water, salt, and olive oil to a boil in nonaluminum stockpot over high heat.
3. Wash parsley, dry with paper towels, and chop enough to measure 1 tablespoon. Set aside.
4. Grate enough Asiago and pecorino Romano to measure ⅓ cup each.
5. Combine grated cheeses in small bowl. Add black pepper to taste and toss with fork to combine.
6. Place 4 dinner plates in oven to warm.
7. Add pasta to boiling water and cook according to package directions until *al dente*. Do not overcook.
8. Turn pasta into colander to drain.
9. Add butter and heavy cream to pot. Add drained pasta and toss gently with 2 wooden spoons until evenly coated. Add half of cheese-pepper mixture and toss to combine.
10. Divide pasta among 4 warm dinner plates, sprinkle with reserved parsley, and serve with remaining cheese on the side.

Braised Romaine Lettuce

3½ cups chicken stock
Large head romaine lettuce (about 2 pounds)
2 cloves garlic
¼ cup olive oil
Salt and freshly ground black pepper

1. Bring chicken stock to a boil in medium-size sauté pan over medium-high heat.
2. Meanwhile, wash lettuce and dry with paper towels. Discard any bruised or discolored leaves and remove spines from outer, less tender leaves.
3. Add spines to boiling stock, lower heat, cover, and simmer 3 minutes.
4. Meanwhile, bruise garlic under flat blade of chef's knife and peel.
5. Add lettuce leaves to stock, pushing down into stock, and return to a boil. Turn off heat and allow lettuce to rest in hot stock, checking texture to prevent overcooking, about 5 minutes.
6. Turn lettuce into strainer set over large bowl and allow to cool 2 to 3 minutes; reserve cooking liquid for another use. Dry sauté pan.
7. Heat olive oil in the sauté pan over medium heat. Add garlic and sauté, stirring occasionally, 2 to 3 minutes, or until golden. Remove garlic and discard.
8. Add lettuce and toss until evenly coated with oil and heated through, about 2 to 3 minutes.
9. Add salt and pepper to taste, divide lettuce among individual plates or bowls, and serve.

Lamb Kidneys Florentine with Saffron Rice
Sicilian Orange Salad

Buy lamb kidneys from a butcher. They should be shiny and semi-firm without any soft spots, and should smell fresh. Kidneys are highly perishable, so store them loosely wrapped in the coldest section of your refrigerator, and use them within two days of purchase.

WHAT TO DRINK

A hearty red wine is needed here. The cooks suggest the fine Lombardy wine provocatively named Inferno. A Gattinara or Ghemme from Piedmont, or any other wine made from the Nebbiolo grape, would also be good.

For an informal meal, mound the rice on a large platter and spoon the kidneys and their sauce on top. The serve-yourself salad is a decorative arrangement of orange slices on a bed of lettuce with Kalamata olives and a garlic vinaigrette.

SHOPPING LIST AND STAPLES

16 lamb kidneys (about 1¼ pounds total weight)
1 head romaine, Boston, or Bibb lettuce
2 medium-size onions
2 bunches fresh parsley
Small bunch fresh rosemary, or ½ teaspoon dried
2 cloves garlic
2 lemons
4 large navel oranges
3½ cups chicken stock, preferably homemade
   (see page 13), approximately, or two 13¾-ounce cans
2½ sticks unsalted butter
2 ounces Asiago cheese, preferably, or Parmesan
½ cup walnut oil, preferably, or olive oil
11-ounce jar Kalamata olives
1½ cups Italian Arborio rice, preferably, or long-grain

Pinch of powdered saffron
Salt and freshly ground black pepper
¼ cup dry Marsala
½ cup dry white wine

UTENSILS

Food processor (optional)
Medium-size heavy-gauge sauté pan or Dutch oven
   with cover
Small saucepan
13 x 9-inch flameproof baking dish
2 large serving platters
Medium-size bowl (if not using processor)
Small bowl
Measuring cups and spoons
Chef's knife
Paring knife
Wooden spoon
Metal tongs
Grater (if not using processor)
Rolling pin
Small glass jar with lid

START-TO-FINISH STEPS

1. Peel and finely chop onions for rice and kidneys recipes. Peel and mince garlic for rice and salad recipes. Wash parsley, and fresh rosemary if using; dry with paper towels. Chop enough parsley to measure ¼ cup for rice, ¾ cup for kidneys, and 2 tablespoons for salad recipes. Chop enough rosemary to measure 1 teaspoon for kidneys recipe. Squeeze enough lemon to measure 1½ tablespoons juice for kidneys recipe and 2 tablespoons for salad recipe.
2. Follow salad recipe steps 1 through 5.
3. Follow rice recipe steps 1 through 6; wash and dry food processor, if using.
4. Follow kidneys recipe steps 1 through 6.
5. Follow rice recipe steps 7 and 8.
6. Follow kidneys recipe step 7.
7. Follow salad recipe step 6, rice recipe step 9, kidneys recipe step 8, and serve.

RECIPES

Lamb Kidneys Florentine with Saffron Rice

16 lamb kidneys (about 1¼ pounds total weight)
1 teaspoon chopped fresh rosemary, or ½ teaspoon dried
1½ sticks unsalted butter, at room temperature
Medium-size onion, finely chopped
¾ cup chopped parsley
1½ tablespoons lemon juice
1 teaspoon salt
¼ teaspoon freshly ground black pepper
¼ cup dry Marsala
Saffron Rice (see following recipe)

1. Preheat broiler.

2. With a very sharp knife, remove outer membrane from each kidney and discard. Halve each kidney lengthwise and cut out white knob in center.

3. If using dried rosemary, crush between 2 sheets of waxed paper with rolling pin.

4. If using food processor, combine rosemary, butter, onion, parsley, lemon juice, salt, and pepper, and process into a paste; do *not* overprocess. Or, combine ingredients in medium-size bowl and blend with back of spoon.

5. With ¼ cup butter mixture, lightly coat bottom of shallow flameproof baking dish just large enough to snugly hold kidney halves in a single layer. Place kidneys cut-side up in the dish, dot with remaining butter mixture, and sprinkle with Marsala.

6. Set broiler rack 4 inches away from heating element and broil kidneys 4 minutes.

7. With metal tongs, turn kidneys; baste generously with pan liquid and broil another 4 minutes, or until browned.

8. Turn kidneys out onto platter on top of Saffron Rice, top with butter sauce, and serve.

Saffron Rice

3½ cups chicken stock, approximately
1 stick unsalted butter
Medium-size onion, finely chopped
1 clove garlic, minced
Pinch of powdered saffron
1½ cups Italian Arborio rice, preferably, or long-grain
½ cup dry white wine
2 ounces Asiago cheese, preferably, or Parmesan
¼ cup finely chopped parsley
Salt and freshly ground black pepper

1. Bring stock to a simmer in small saucepan over high heat.

2. Meanwhile, melt 4 tablespoons butter in medium-size heavy-gauge sauté pan or Dutch oven over medium heat. Add onion and garlic, and sauté about 5 minutes, or until onion is soft and translucent.

3. In small bowl, combine saffron with 2 tablespoons hot stock and stir until dissolved.

4. Add rice to sauté pan and sauté, stirring, 2 minutes.

5. Stir in 3 cups stock, wine, and dissolved saffron, and bring to a boil over medium heat. Cover, reduce heat, and simmer gently about 20 minutes.

6. Using food processor or grater, grate enough cheese to measure ½ cup. Cut remaining butter into small pieces.

7. Place large serving platter under hot water to warm.

8. Check rice for tenderness. If liquid is absorbed before rice is cooked, add small amount of remaining hot stock, cover, and continue cooking. Or, if rice is cooked before liquid has been absorbed, remove cover, raise heat to medium, and boil off excess liquid, being careful not to burn rice.

9. Dry platter. With fork, stir in cheese, pieces of butter, and parsley, and fluff rice. Add salt and pepper to taste, and turn rice out onto warm serving platter.

Sicilian Orange Salad

1 head romaine, Boston, or Bibb lettuce
½ cup walnut oil, preferably, or olive oil
2 tablespoons lemon juice
1 clove garlic, minced
Salt and freshly ground black pepper
4 large navel oranges
8 Kalamata olives
2 tablespoons chopped parsley

1. Wash and dry lettuce. Remove any bruised or discolored leaves. Line serving platter with lettuce.

2. Combine oil, lemon juice, garlic, and salt and pepper to taste in small jar with lid or other container and shake until blended.

3. With sharp paring knife, peel oranges, removing as much of white pith as possible. Cut crosswise into ½-inch-thick slices.

4. Remove pits from olives and cut each olive lengthwise into quarters.

5. Top lettuce with orange slices, overlapping slices slightly. Sprinkle with olives, cover with plastic wrap, and refrigerate until ready to serve.

6. Just before serving, shake dressing to recombine and pour over salad. Sprinkle with parsley.

ADDED TOUCH

Zabaglione is an egg custard that can be served warm or cold. Top it with berries or chocolate shavings.

Zabaglione

1 pint fresh raspberries or strawberries (optional)
½ cup Grand Marnier or other orange-flavored liqueur (if using berries)
6 egg yolks
5 tablespoons superfine sugar
⅔ cup dry Marsala
1 ounce shaved bittersweet chocolate (if *not* using berries)

1. Gently rinse berries, if using, and dry with paper towels. Hull berries.

2. Combine berries and liqueur in medium-size bowl and gently toss until berries are well-coated; set aside to macerate 15 to 20 minutes at room temperature.

3. Off heat, whisk egg yolks in top of double boiler or in heatproof bowl until yolks fall from whisk in ribbons.

4. Gradually add sugar and Marsala, whisking after each addition, until incorporated.

5. Cook mixture over, not in, barely simmering water, whisking constantly and occasionally scraping down sides of pan or bowl, about 10 minutes, or until mixture thickens, fluffs up, and holds its shape in a spoon. Do *not* overcook.

6. With slotted spoon, divide berries, if using, among bowls and top with zabaglione. Or, divide zabaglione among bowls and top each serving with shaved chocolate.

Acknowledgments

Our special thanks to the International Olive Oil Council for their assistance in the preparation of this volume.

The Editors would like to thank the following for their courtesy in lending items for photography: *Cover:* tiles—Elon Tiles, Inc. *Frontispiece:* cheese tray—The Mediterranean Shop; white plate—Buffalo China; canister—courtesy of Giuliano Bugialli; ladle—Linda Campbell Franklin Collection. *Page 18–19:* plate—Pottery Barn; salad bowl, platter—Dan Bleier; glasses—Gorham. *Page 22:* round plate—Pottery Barn; square plate—Julien Mousa-Oghli; paper surface—Four Hands Bindery; fork—The Lauffer Co. *Page 24:* plates—Mark Anderson; fork—Wallace Silversmiths. *Pages 26–27:* plates—MacKenzie-Childs, Ltd.; utensils—Gorham. *Page 30:* dishes—Villeroy & Boch; servers—The Lauffer Co.; tablecloth—Conran's; napkin—Leacock & Co. *Page 34–35:* platters, pitcher—Deruta of Italy, Co. *Page 38:* dishes—Haviland & Co.; flatware—Gorham. *Page 41:* flatware—Gorham; plates, checked cloth, glass—Pottery Barn. *Page 44–45:* pasta bowl—Prestilo, courtesy of Of All Things; napkin—Of All Things. *Page 48:* platters—Deruta of Italy, Co. *Page 51:* plates—

Conran's. *Pages 54–55:* tiles—Elon Tiles, Inc.; platters—Mud, Sweat & Tears. *Pages 58–59:* plates—The Mediterranean Shop. *Page 61:* plates—Conran's; flatware—The Lauffer Co. *Pages 64–65:* plates—Dorothy Hafner; flatware—Wallace Silversmiths; glasses—Pottery Barn; napkin—The Leacock Co. *Page 68:* servers—Lauffer & Co.; platters—The Mediterranean Shop. *Page 71:* paper surface—Four Hands Bindery; flatware—Wallace Silversmiths. *Pages 74–75:* marble, napkin—Pottery Barn. *Page 78:* tiles—Country Floors, Inc.; plate—Wolfman-Gold & Good Co. *Page 81:* basket—Be Seated, Inc.; salad bowl—Wolfman-Gold & Good Co.; platter—Villeroy & Boch; tiles—Country Floors, Inc. *Pages 84–85:* dishes—Siena by Villeroy & Boch; mat—Ad Hoc Housewares; flatware—Gorham; black plates—Of All Things. *Page 91:* tablecloth—Conran's; beige platter, salad bowl, black servers—Ad Hoc Housewares; iron bowls, stainless utensils, frog—Sointu. *Pages 94–95:* salad bowls, service plates—Ad Hoc Housewares; tiles—Amaru's Tiles; glass—Gorham; basket—Be Seated. *Page 98:* plate—Pan American Phoenix; napkin—Ad Hoc Softwares; glass—Conran's. *Pages 100–101:* tiles—Country Floors, Inc.; platters—Buffalo China.

Kitchen equipment courtesy of: White-Westinghouse, Commercial Aluminum Cookware Co., Robot-Coupe, Caloric, Kitchen-Aid, J.A. Henckels Zwillingswerk, Inc., and Schwabel Corp. Microwave oven compliments of Litton Microwave Cooking Products.

Illustrations by Ray Skibinski
Production by Giga Communications

Mail-Order Sources for Quail

Czimer Foods, Inc.
Route No. 7, Box 285
Lockport, IL 60441
(312) 460-2210

The Forst's
CPO Box 1000P
12–24 Ten Broeck Ave.
Kingston, NY 12401
(914) 331-3500

Quail Roost Quail Farms
8942 SW 129 Terrace
Miami, FL 33176
(305) 253-8319

Index

Time-Life Books Inc. offers a wide
range of fine recordings, including
a Big Band series. For subscription
information, call 1-800-621-7026, or
write TIME-LIFE MUSIC, Time & Life
Building, Chicago, Illinois 60611.